THE FLORIDA KEYS
VOLUME 2

True Stories of the Perilous Straits

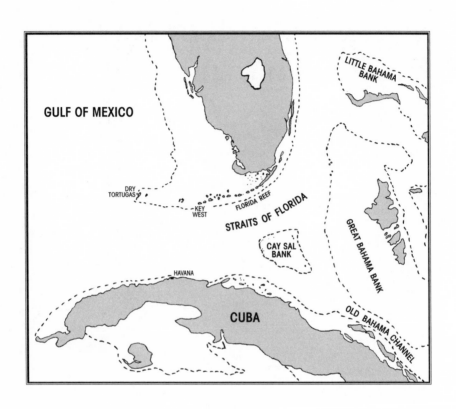

THE FLORIDA KEYS

VOLUME 2

True Stories of the Perilous Straits

John Viele

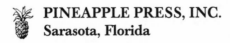

PINEAPPLE PRESS, INC.
Sarasota, Florida

Inquiries should be addressed to:
Pineapple Press, Inc.
P.O. Box 3889
Sarasota, Florida 34230
www.pineapplepress.com

LIBRARY OF CONGRESS
CATALOGING-IN-PUBLICATION DATA

Viele, John, 1923–
        The Florida keys volume 2 : true stories of the perilous straits
/ John Viele. – 1st ed.
        p.   cm. – (Florida's history through its places)
        Includes bibliographical references and index.
        ISBN 1-56164-179-0 (alk. paper)
        1. Florida Keys (Fla.)—History. 2. Florida Keys (Fla.)—Social
life and customs. 3. Florida Keys (Fla.)—Biography. I. Title. II. Series
F317.M7V54   1996
975.9'41—dc20   95-50036

First Edition
10 9 8 7 6 5 4 3

Design by Carol Tornatore
Composition by Stacey Arnold
Printed in the United States of America

To Ann, Pete, Tom, Phyllis, Ginger,
and my beloved helpmate, Pam

Contents

Acknowledgments

Of the many people and organizations who helped me with the research for this book, none is more deserving of my thanks than Gail Swanson of Grassy Key, Florida. Her painstaking research into the history of the Florida Keys before 1800, which she willingly shared with me, provided me with, or led me to, primary sources for a number of the stories in Chapters 2, 3 and 4. In particular, her research furnished material for the stories of Britton Hammon, HMS *Tyger,* and the *Polly and Nancy.* My sincere thanks also go to Jim Clupper, manager of the Helen Wadley Branch Library, Islamorada, Florida, another dedicated Keys history researcher, who freely shared his discoveries and knowledge with me. I am deeply grateful to Dr. Eugene Lyon, Director of the Center for Historic Research at Flagler College, St. Augustine, for taking much of his valuable time to share his knowledge of the history of Keys natives and to translate Spanish archival documents concerning the employment of Keys natives as salvage divers by Spanish salvage expeditions.

The staff of a number of libraries and archives were most helpful to me in my research. I especially wish to thank the staff of the Monroe County Public Library, Key West, in particular, Tom Hambright, Director of the Florida History Department and his assistant Lynda Hambright; as well as Cynthia Lawson and Mary Ann Duchardt of the Reference Department. The staff of the Mariners' Museum Research Library, Newport News, Virginia, especially Heather Friedle, could not have been more helpful.

Andrea Cordani, a private research consultant in London, England, made it possible to put the complete story of HMS *Tyger* together by finding copies of the ship's log and the court-martial testimony in the Public Record Office. She also gave me valuable leads for finding paintings of the *Tyger* and helped me understand the mysteries of British Royal Navy record keeping in the eighteenth century.

I was most fortunate to be made aware of the talents of a self-taught artist at the Pigeon Key National Historic Site. Often working from little more than verbal descriptions, Wayne Giordano was able to recreate realistic scenes of Keys natives, pirates, and sea fights. Another talented Keys artist, Naya Rydzewski of Cudjoe Key, produced a fine watercolor of the revenue cutter *Campbell* establishing a base on Tea Table Key during the Second Seminole War. I also wish to express my appreciation to Jim Lloyd, a retired designer, who contributed two fine drawings for the story of the ill-fated missionary expedition to the Calusa.

In my search for illustrations, I was greatly assisted by the staff of the photographic department at Mariners' Museum, Newport News. Claudia Jew, Assistant Manager, Photographic Services, offered useful suggestions on illustration sources and facilitated my order for photographs in many ways. Joan Morris, director of the photographic collection at the Florida State Archives in Tallahassee, went out of her way to find the illustrations for which I was searching. Adolph Gucinski, contract photographer for the Monroe County Public Library, reproduced prints from the library's collection with unfailing high quality. Finally, I thank Fred Courtright of W. W. Norton Co. for obtaining permission for me to reproduce two drawings by Henry Rusk of revenue cutters from Howard I. Chapelle's *The History of American Sailing Ships*.

Introduction

*T*his is the second in a series of books on the history of the Florida Keys. The first volume, *The Florida Keys: A History of the Pioneers,* presents stories of the rugged men and women who struggled to make a life for themselves on the isolated and often hostile Keys as far back as the Native Americans who lived there a thousand or more years ago. The second volume covers the maritime history of the Keys and the Straits of Florida from the time of the aboriginal natives in the early 1500s to the end of the Second Seminole War in 1842. A third volume, now under preparation, tells the story of the wreck salvaging industry which began even before Key West was settled and brought great wealth to the city.

The Straits of Florida are a 110-mile sea passage between the Gulf of Mexico and the Atlantic Ocean bordered on the northern side by the Florida Keys and the Florida Reef. The passage has been called one of the most dangerous in the world. In its waters, along the reef, and on desolate keys, thousands of men and women have died in shipwrecks, attacks by natives, sea battles, and pirate boardings. Few of their stories have survived, but those that have tell gripping tales of their struggles against the perils of the sea and the onslaughts of men. This book presents a selection of such stories during the age of sail from the time Spanish navigators discovered the Straits to the end of the Second Seminole War in 1842. The stories include accounts of castaway mariners, native divers, privateersmen, and pirates. There are tales of revenue marines patrolling the Keys to apprehend pirates and smugglers, and of sailors and marines hunting the elusive Seminole Indians in the Keys and the Everglades.

Wherever possible, the stories are taken from original sources such as ships' logs, captains' journals, letters, and court records. Secondary sources include newspaper articles and government reports and records of the times.

In the Straits of Florida, the swift eastward-flowing Florida Current (commonly called the Gulf Stream) combines with hidden reefs on both sides to make navigation a challenge even for modern mariners. In the days of sail, when ships were at the mercy of wind and current, when there were no lighthouses along the reef, when charts were grossly inaccurate, and when navigators had only the crudest means of determining their position, a successful passage was as much a matter of good fortune as it was of skill. In 1842, *Hunt's Merchant's Magazine and Commercial Review* said, "There is no portion of the American coast more dangerous to the mariner, or where more property is annually wrecked, than on the Florida Reef."

Proceeding from the Gulf of Mexico, the passage through the Straits of Florida begins in the vicinity of the Dry Tortugas, a group of small low-lying keys some seventy miles to the west of Key West. The passage runs eastward and then gradually curves to the north as it rounds the Florida Keys. This curvature of the route posed an additional problem for early navigators who, up until the late 1700s, had no means of accurately determining their longitude (east-west position).

1715 map of the Caribbean by geographer Herman Moll showing Straits of Florida and tracks of Spanish treasure fleets (from an engraving in the collection of Historic Urban Plans, Inc., Ithaca, NY)

The Straits are approximately ninety miles wide in the vicinity of Key West, gradually narrowing to about forty-five miles off the southern Florida mainland. The southern and western sides of the Strait are bordered by the northern coast of Cuba, Cay Sal Bank, Great Bahama Bank, and Little Bahama Bank. Even though the Keys are low lying and fronted by a dangerous reef, sailing ship captains preferred to keep to the Florida side of the Straits because the passage was shorter and because landmarks, so essential to early navigators, are scarce along the edge of the Cay Sal and Bahama banks. Ships bound through the Straits from the Atlantic to the Gulf of Mexico also chose to stay close to the Keys to avoid stemming the Florida Current as much as possible.

At the northern exit of the Straits, the Florida Current combines with the Antilles Current to form the Gulf Stream. In the center of the Straits, the current flows at speeds of up to four miles per hour. It was not unusual, in light airs, for sailing ships bound to the Gulf of Mexico to find themselves moving backwards. The position of the current is not stationary. It meanders from side to side and sometimes even flows in over the Florida Reef. Along the edge of the reef, there may be a counter current, but it is not predictable. In 1836, the *Key West Inquirer* reported, "It is unusual for us to announce so many wrecks as have recently occurred in so short a time, unless after some great and disastrous gale. These however have happened in consequence of a severe current setting directly upon the Florida Reef. Its rapidity has been estimated from 3 to 3 1/2 miles per hour. And when vessels once get on the coral reef with this current, it is difficult, if not impossible, to get off without the assistance of lighters [usually wrecking vessels which offloaded cargo]."

While the prevailing winds in the Straits are from the southeast, there are extended periods of calm in the summer and dangerous frontal passages bringing gale force winds in the winter. In the hurricane season, there is a high probability of such storms crossing the Straits, and many have done so with disastrous results to shipping.

Rainfall in the Keys is limited to about forty inches annually, and only a few of the islands have sinkholes where castaway mariners could find fresh water. Until the middle of the eighteenth century, the Keys were peopled by hostile natives who often murdered or enslaved castaway seamen.

Despite the many perils, the Straits of Florida offered the best and fastest passage between the Gulf of Mexico and the Atlantic. Beginning with the transit of the first Spanish treasure ship in 1519, the Straits became the favored route for all maritime traffic leaving the Gulf of Mexico and the western Caribbean, from as far away as Jamaica. As early as 1697, an English convoy from Jamaica passing through the Straits numbered 116 merchant ships escorted by six warships. By the middle of the first half of the nineteenth century, Stephen R. Mallory, a U.S. senator and a native of Key West, was able to say, "There is scarcely a day . . . that you may not see in the business season from 100 to 150 square-rigged vessels entering or leaving the Gulf [In the 1800s, Keys mariners referred to the Straits of Florida as the Gulf.]."

The rich cargoes of this traffic soon attracted pirates and privateers, and, as ships piled up on the reef in ever increasing numbers, salvage hunters (or, as they came to be known, wreckers). The commercial opportunities provided by the parade of ships passing the Keys and the wrecks left in their wake led to the founding of Key West in 1822. As previously noted, the story of the wrecking industry and the daring exploits of the wreckers will be related in a subsequent volume in this series.

With a deep-water harbor directly on a major shipping lane and capital generated by the lucrative wrecking business, Key West soon developed into a major seaport. Recognizing its strategic location at the gateway to the Gulf of Mexico, the Navy established a base at Key West which, with brief interruptions, has remained there to this day. In the beginning, it served as a depot for the antipiracy squadron under Commodore Porter. He extolled its advantages as a naval station, saying that it had no equal except Gibraltar.

A totally new and different role for naval forces arose during the Second Seminole War (1836–1842). At bases in the upper Keys, sailors and marines trained to fire small arms and handle dugout canoes, and then sailed to the mainland to hunt down Seminole Indians hidden in the vast watery wilderness of the Everglades.

From native treasure divers to seagoing Indian hunters, these are tales of men's courage, cruelty, and suffering as they fought the elements and each other in the waters along the Florida Keys.

NOTE: A glossary of nautical terms is supplied at the end of the last chapter.

THE FLORIDA KEYS
VOLUME 2

True Stories of the Perilous Straits

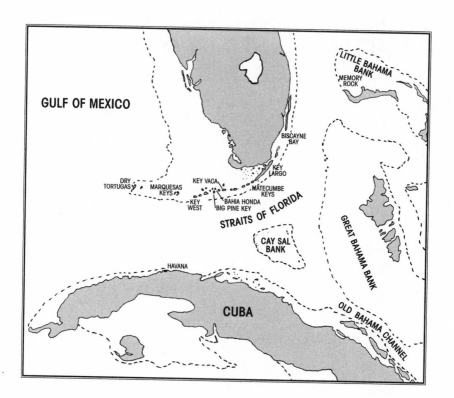

Chapter 1

SEAGOING NATIVES

Voyages by Dugout

*T*he first vessels to ply the waters along the Florida Reef were the dugout canoes of the Keys natives. Estimates of the beginning of human occupation of the Keys range from one thousand to three thousand years ago. These original inhabitants were hunter-gatherers. Much of their food and most of their tools, implements, and weapons—made from seashells and fish bones—came from the sea. Of necessity, they were skilled mariners. From pine or cypress logs, they hollowed out canoes ranging in length from ten to forty or more feet. Individuals or families used the smaller dugouts to fish and gather shellfish and to move from island to island. Warriors used the larger dugouts for war and for trade with distant tribes on the mainland. To transport large cargoes, the natives sometimes lashed two dugouts together with a platform across them to form a sort of catamaran.

In the 1500s, Spanish fishermen from Havana regularly fished the rich waters around the Keys and traded with the natives. Writing in 1570, a Spanish historian reported that the Los Cayos (Keys) Indians traveled between the islands in dugout canoes and *chalupas* (shallops—small, undecked sailing craft). Use of the term *chalupa* indicates that the natives were building larger dugouts and had adopted the use of sails from their contacts with the Cuban fishing vessels.

Documents in Spanish archives show that Keys natives routinely made coastal voyages of several hundred miles in their dugouts. In 1605, Matecumbe natives told the crew of a stranded Spanish vessel that they were accustomed to voyaging to St. Augustine, a distance of more than four hundred miles. The following story illustrates the extensive intertribal and intervillage travel and communication that existed in south Florida and the Keys in the late seventeenth century.

A Harrowing Voyage to the Keys

In a letter written to the King of Spain in 1634, a friar in Havana advised that reports from Spanish vessels touching the Keys and south coasts of Florida indicated that the Indians of Carlos (the Calusa in the Charlotte Harbor area), Posoy (in Tampa Bay area), and Matecumbe (in the Keys) would welcome missionaries.

The friar urged the King to authorize missions to these Indians, arguing that their conversion to Christianity would help save the lives of castaway seamen. Despite his plea, more than sixty years were to pass before a missionary effort was made in south Florida.

Efforts to organize a mission to the south Florida Indians were revived in the 1680s. In 1689, the Bishop of Cuba invited the chief of the Calusa (a tribe on the southwest coast of Florida) to Havana for a visit. Brought there by a fishing vessel, the chief was persuaded to ask for baptism and to offer all his subjects for conversion to Christianity.

Eight years passed before the funds and volunteer Franciscan friars were ready for a "harvest of souls" among the Calusa. On September 11, 1697, five friars under the leadership of Feliciano López departed Havana onboard a fishing sloop, carrying with them provisions and other supplies sufficient for six months. The story of this ill-fated mission is derived from testimony given by the friars and other persons who were involved after they had returned to Havana five months later. Documents containing their sworn statements were translated by John H. Hann and published in his book, *Missions to the Calusa*. Because of a number of inconsistencies and conflicts in the statements, the story that follows must be considered an estimate of what actually happened.

One and a half days after leaving Havana, the sloop dropped anchor in the harbor of the Key of Bones (Key West) and remained there for two days. During this time, the friars undoubtedly met with the chief of the Key of Bones and very likely discussed with him the possibility of his accepting missionaries.

After a four-day voyage up the west coast of Florida, the sloop arrived off Key Carlos (believed to be a small key in the vicinity of Estero Bay, possibly what is known as Mound Key today). The Calusa were the most powerful tribe in south Florida and were fierce warriors. The captain of the sloop, Francisco Romero, anchored well offshore because of his fear of these Indians. But his fears proved groundless. A young chief, heir apparent of the Calusa nation, came out to the sloop and welcomed the friars. The following day, the natives carried the missionaries and their supplies ashore. When the sloop was ready to leave, Friar López asked a seventeen-year old crewman, Juan Esteva, to remain with the missionaries to act as their servant. Esteva agreed.

The missionaries stayed in the house of the old chief, Chief Carlos, leader of the Calusa, until they had finished building a combined house and church for themselves. They used logs and palm fronds provided by the Indians in exchange for gifts of maize and tobacco. When the friars moved to their new home, the Indians asked why they took their supplies with them instead of distributing them to the members of the tribe.

It soon became apparent that the Indians' only interest in becoming Christians was the food, clothing, and other gifts the friars had to offer. When the friars refused to give them more, they became sullen and angry. When the friars attempted to invade the Indians' temple in order to destroy their idols, the Indians drove the friars away with blows and threats to kill them. As the days wore on, the situation continued to deteriorate. The Indians stole supplies from the friars' house and became increasingly hostile. One native rubbed a friar's face with feces; another urinated on a friar as he was kneeling in prayer. Only the intercession of the old chief—who warned his tribe that if they harmed the friars, the Spanish would send soldiers to punish them—prevented the warriors from carrying out their threats to kill the missionaries.

After two months, with the old chief now dead, the young chief told the friars they must leave. His brother, known as the "Great Captain," had, on several occasions, protected the friars. He warned Friar López, "Did I not tell you, Father, that this cacique [the young chief] was so evil a man? Go quickly, because if you do not, they are going to kill you."

The young chief told the friars that they should go to the Key of Bones and wait there for a passing vessel to take them back to Havana. He would provide a dugout canoe and an Indian escort to take them there.

In order to be able to carry all their provisions, clothing, religious items, and other supplies, the friars lashed two small fishing dugouts together and placed a platform across them to form a crude catamaran. Their young servant, Esteva, loaded the catamaran with three bushels of maize, bundles of clothing, and other items. As soon as he had finished loading, several Indians stole the catamaran. The young chief ordered some Indians to carry the friars' supplies down to the shore, but on the way they fled into the woods with their loads. The friars and Esteva managed to save only the things they carried themselves.

On December 2, the five friars embarked in a large dugout canoe manned by the Great Captain, the chief of the Muspa (a subgroup of the Calusa, two days' journey south of Key Carlos), and two Calusa Indians, making a total of nine. Esteva somehow managed to obtain another small fishing dugout, and, after loading it with several jugs of honey, wine, and sugar, paddled it by himself. One of the curious aspects of the friars' narratives, given after their return to Havana, is that they never mention Esteva despite the fact that he was with them for the entire time and underwent the same trials and sufferings. It would appear that they did not consider a servant worthy of notice.

Throughout the ensuing voyage, the Indians followed an inside route through the many keys that line the southwest coast in order to remain in sheltered water and to avoid any passing Spanish vessels. The first day, they traveled only a short distance. Along the way, Esteva was stopped by a passing dugout manned by four Indian men and two Indian women, and they took one of his jugs of honey. That evening, after the dugouts were pulled up on a beach, the Indians helped themselves to the wine and got drunk.

The hungover natives were not ready to get under way for the next village, Teyú, until noon the following day. Teyú was located at the mouth of a river or inlet about twenty miles south of Key Carlos, probably in the vicinity of present-day Naples. Esteva, able to make faster progress in the small dugout, arrived first. The large dugout did not arrive until nightfall. To keep warm in the cold air, as well as to protect their possessions, the friars and Esteva slept in the large dugout, which was tied to the bank. Near morning, two of the friars went ashore to warm themselves by a fire.

At dawn, the friars' Indian escorts swam up to the large dugout and began to untie it. Friar López awoke and attempted to stop them. The Indians tipped the dugout and López fell into the river. Then they threw the other two friars and Esteva into the water. The water was deep and the current strong. Esteva and the two friars managed to paddle to shallow water, but López could not swim. Believing his end was near, he called out "Give me absolution!" Hearing his cry, the two friars by the fire ran to the river bank. Seizing a long stick of wood, they waded into the water and pulled López to safety.

In the meantime, the Indians, after throwing the religious items overboard, took both dugouts with all the friars' remaining provisions and clothing and paddled away. Only the Great Captain did not participate in the theft. Throughout the commotion, he lay on the ground feigning sleep.

The Indian escorts tipped over the dugout canoe, throwing Friar López into the water
(drawing by Jim Lloyd)

7

The missionaries and their servant remained by the river all that day and night pondering their next move. Perhaps they were reassured by the Great Captain that the rest of their escort would return.

Two hours before dawn, while the friars were warming themselves by the fire, a party of Indians from Teyú appeared carrying arrows and spears. Fearful of being attacked, the friars and their servant, accompanied by the Great Captain, left the campsite and began walking along the beach to get past the village of Teyú. Later in the morning, they sighted the large dugout, paddled by the chief of the Muspa and the two Calusa Indians, returning to pick them up. When they reboarded, they noted that the only supplies left were four or five sacks of maize, one sack of biscuit, and a little box of religious books.

That evening, they arrived at the village of Muspa, located on a large key in the vicinity of Cape Romano. On the way, the chief of Muspa and the two Calusa stripped the friars of their habits, shoes, and stockings, leaving them clothed in only their undershirts and linen breeches. The chief of Muspa told the friars that they should stay at Muspa until the chief of the

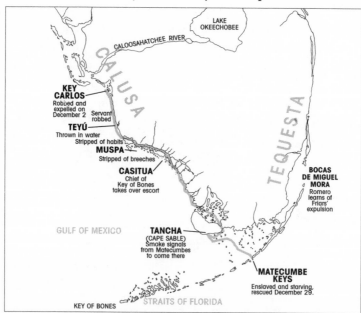

Map of route from Key Carlos to Matecumbe Key followed by Indians carrying friars and their servant in dugout canoes in 1697

Key of Bones, who had gone to Carlos to pick them up, arrived. It was evident that news of the friars' expulsion had traveled all the way down the coast to the keys. But there was no explanation as to why the chief of the Key of Bones had undertaken a journey of two hundred miles to pick up the friars. As the Keys Indians were subject to the Calusa, it is possible that the chief of the Key of Bones had been summoned to rid the Calusa of their unwelcome guests, but when the old chief, Carlos, died, the young chief decided he could wait no longer and sent the friars on their way.

As it happened, the missionary party spent only one day and night at Muspa. In the morning, the chief of Muspa sent the friars and their servant off with four Muspa Indians as escort. There is no indication of the reason for the change in plans. The best guess is that news had arrived that the chief of the Key of Bones had not yet begun his trip to Carlos.

The new escort was no improvement over the previous one. On the way to the next village south, Casitua, the Muspa Indians took the friars' cowls and breeches, leaving them shivering in nothing more than their undershirts. They also took Esteva's breeches, but gave him some torn breeches of "hemp" (possibly palm fronds or grass) to replace them.

Casitua, described in Spanish documents as the next village south of Muspa, may have been located in the vicinity of Everglades City. The friars waited there for ten days until the chief of the Key of Bones, accompanied by two of his subjects, arrived. With the friars and Esteva in their dugout, the Key of Bones escort began paddling south.

The next stop was the village of Tancha, situated at Cape Sable, some fifty miles distant from Casitua. While there, the Indians would occasionally give the friars a little bit of fish to eat and forced Esteva to go with them in their dugouts to catch the fish. After several days, smoke signals from the Matecumbe Keys forty miles away told the Indians they should come. The Tancha Indians, with their families, departed first. Then the Key of Bones escort carried the friars and Esteva across Florida Bay to Matecumbe and abandoned them.

In the meantime, the authorities at Havana (unaware of the mission's situation) had dispatched two different vessels to deliver messages to Friar López in order to find out how the mission was faring and to provide any needed assistance. One of these was the same fishing sloop that had taken the friars to Key Carlos, captained by the same pilot, Francisco Romero. Instead of going directly to Key Carlos, Romero, apparently more interested in fishing than in delivering messages, went to the Keys. From the Matecumbe Indians he learned of the mission's expulsion. At the "Mouths" (Bocas de Miguel Mora, the entrance to Biscayne Bay just south of Key Biscayne), he met an Indian from Carlos, who also reported the friars' departure from Carlos and said he was returning there. Romero gave him a message for Friar López and warned him that the Indians would be punished if any harm came to the priests. By way of reply, the Indian laughed at him.

The Matecumbe Indians, although reported to have been converted to Christianity, took no pity on the friars. Seeing them nearly naked, dressed only in their "little" undershirts, the Indians concluded that their gods had deserted them. They not only would give them nothing to eat, but forced them to serve as slaves by having them carry jugs of water. During the time (approximately a week) they were on Matecumbe, the friars and Esteva barely managed to stay alive by eating raw shellfish.

On December 29, four weeks after they left Key Carlos, the friars and Esteva were rescued. On his return from the Mouths, Romero sailed to the Matecumbe Keys and sighted the friars on the beach searching for shellfish. Friar López and one of the other friars paddled slowly out to the sloop in a dugout. Their undershirts were so worn and torn that their skin showed through. They were badly sunburned and very weak. When the sailors gave them a little biscuit soaked in wine and a bit of chocolate, they promptly threw it up.

The friars' ordeal was not completely finished. The sailors gave them clothes from their meager stores and shared their food with them, but for almost two more months, the friars were forced to live in the cramped quarters of the sloop while Romero and his crew continued fishing. Finally, on February 21, 1698, they returned to Havana and prepared to give their testimony on the failure of the mission to the Calusa.

Crossing the Straits

At the end of the seventeenth century, south Florida natives, including those in the Keys, were crossing the Straits of Florida to trade with the

Spanish in Havana. According to Barcia's *Chronological History of the Continent of Florida,* written in the early 1700s, the natives voyaged from the Keys to Havana (a distance of ninety miles) in twenty-four hours. They could not have made such crossings without the use of sails, and it is possible they used

Artist's concept of a dugout catamaran that might have been
used by Keys natives to cross the Straits of Florida to Havana
in the late 1600s (drawing by Jim Lloyd)

two dugouts lashed together to provide greater stability and sea worthiness.

On arrival in Havana, the south Florida natives traded fish, ambergris, tree bark, fruit, and hides for rum, tobacco, sugar, knives, and other European items. An unusual and highly profitable trade good was the cardinal. Spanish seamen prized these birds as pets and paid high prices for them. A report written from Havana in 1689 states, "When the fleet [treasure fleet] was sailing, the trade in cardinal birds was substantial. . . ."

A French priest who was shipwrecked in the Keys in 1722 encountered a band of Keys natives. One of their leaders told him that nearly all the members of his village had been baptized as Catholics in Havana, and that they voyaged there once a year. The priest said they made such voyages in dugout canoes which he described as "small, very flat pirogues, in which we [Frenchmen] should hardly trust ourselves across the Seine at Paris."

The Keys natives of the late 1600s had neither compasses nor charts nor access to weather predictions, and they knew little or nothing about currents. Yet in open dugouts rigged with primitive sails, they crossed the ninety miles of open water that separate the Keys from Cuba. Such voyages demonstrate that they possessed remarkable seamanship and navigation skills as well as considerable courage.

The First Wreckers

The usual image of wreck salvaging in the Keys is one of fast sloops and schooners, manned by daring Bahamian and American seamen, racing through towering seas and gale winds to an unfortunate ship pounding to pieces on the reef. But in fact, Keys natives, paddling out to the reef in dugout canoes, were plundering wrecks three hundred years before Bahamians and Americans arrived on the scene.

The shipwrecked French priest previously mentioned said that the key on which he landed was devoid of trees and four-footed animals, and that the natives subsisted entirely on seafood. He concluded that the only reason the natives remained on the barren island was to plunder shipwrecks.

When the natives sighted a wreck on the reef, they would paddle out to investigate. They quickly learned that gold, silver, and jewels were valuable not only as adornments but also as barter they could use in trade with other tribes and with Europeans. They also discovered the intoxicating effects of wine and rum, and the usefulness of metal tools such as the hatchets and knives they salvaged from wrecks.

Keys Natives investigating a wreck on reef (drawing by Wayne Giordano)

As early as 1528, natives in the Tampa Bay area were showing members of the Narváez expedition items that had been plundered from shipwrecks. A young boy, Hernando d'Escalante Fontaneda, shipwrecked in the Keys in 1549, wrote that the Indians of Guarugumbe (described by a sixteenth-century Spanish geographer as "on the point of the Martyrs [Keys]") were "rich; but, in the way that I have stated, from the sea [wrecks], not from the land."

In 1592, English privateers under Christopher Newport stopped in the Keys to look for fresh water. The natives told the sailors where they could find water and traded gold and silver they had taken from wrecks for rusty hatchets and knives.

Native Salvage Divers

Having discovered that fascinating and useful items could be found in the cabins and holds of wrecks that were above water, it was not long before the Keys natives began diving into wrecks that were partially or totally submerged. Diving was nothing new to them. In the crystal-clear waters of the Keys, they would dive to pick up shellfish and spear turtles and lobsters. The Spanish geographer, López de Velasco, writing in the 1570s, stated that the natives of south Florida caught manatees by looping a rope around their necks, jumping on their backs, and driving stakes into their nostrils. They would hang on until the animals were exhausted and surfaced. By the early 1600s, the natives had become accomplished salvage divers.

Two of the worst disasters to Spanish treasure fleets took place in the Florida Keys, the first in 1622 and the second in 1733. Native divers from the Keys were employed by the Spanish salvage expeditions in both instances.

The 1622 disaster occurred when a violent hurricane struck a large convoy returning to Spain two days after leaving Havana. Nine of these ships wrecked in the Keys, including the three treasure-carrying galleons *Nuestra Señora de Atocha, Santa Margarita,* and *Nuestra Señora del Rosario.* The *Rosario* went ashore in the Dry Tortugas but did not sink. Her passengers and crew were saved and her treasure salvaged. The *Atocha* and *Santa Margarita* sank in the Quicksands area to the west of the Marquesas Keys.

Hurricanes in 1622 and 1733 struck homeward-bound Spanish treasure fleets in the Straits of Florida, leaving many of the ships wrecked on the Florida Reef (*Galleons in a Tempest, L'Art Des Armées Navales*. From the collections of The Mariners' Museum, Newport News, Virginia)

Only five men survived from the *Atocha* and just sixty-eight from the *Santa Margarita*. In all, 550 lives were lost from the 1622 fleet.

From 1622 to 1643, Spanish expeditions operating from camps on the Marquesas Keys searched the waters to the west of the Keys trying to locate and salvage treasure from the *Atocha* and the *Santa Margarita*. The first expedition reached the Marquesas Keys just ten days after the disaster only to find that Keys natives had already recovered some items from the wrecks. The Spanish were forced to bargain with the natives to get them back.

For the next three years, the Spanish salvors had little success. Finally, in 1626, using a bronze diving bell with glass viewing ports, they located the *Santa Margarita* in about twenty-five feet of water. Concerned that the natives who came to watch in their dugouts might interfere with the recovery work, the Spanish promised to bring them gifts of clothes, hatchets, and liquor. But when the salvors returned the next year, they found their salvage camp and supplies burned to ashes.

In 1628, rather than try to placate the watching natives with gifts, the Spanish salvage master, Francisco Nuñez Melián, put them to work. Having observed that the natives could dive deeper and stay down longer than the Spanish divers, he employed nine Keys native divers along with some pearl divers from the island of Margarita off the coast of Venezuela. Melián paid the divers regularly in coins, and they recovered thirty-seven silver ingots and a large quantity of coins. Before they could bring up more, the Spaniards' enemies, the Dutch, arrived on the scene and forced the salvage party to flee for safety.

In the 1670s, another Spanish salvor, Martín de Melgar, led a number of salvage expeditions to the Bahamas to recover treasure from the wreck of the galleon *Maravillas,* lost near Memory Rock on the edge of Little Bahama Bank. Unable to find enough divers in Cuba to do the work, he followed Melían's example and came to the Keys. On his 1676 expedition, Melgar visited native villages in Key West, Big Pine Key, and Key Vaca to convince native divers to come with him, but he was unsuccessful. Finally, at Matecumbe, with the aid of gifts of liquor, hatchets, knives, cloth, and beads, he persuaded the native chief, Cacique Don Rodrigo, to let him hire three divers, two canoes, and a fisherman to help feed them. He was able to recruit six more divers and a native fisherman from Cacique Don Joseph, chief of a village on Biscayne Bay.

By that time, the Keys natives, as a result of many years of contact with Spanish fishermen from Cuba, had acquired a thin veneer of Spanish culture. Most of the adult males spoke rudimentary Spanish, and many had been baptized in Cuba and had adopted Spanish names. One of the divers from Biscayne Bay, Manuel Mariquin, was described as "a son of the church," probably meaning he had been baptized in Havana. Another diver, Antonio Sanchez, was described as the son of Pedro Sanchez, born in

Keys native diver recovering coins from a sunken Spanish galleon
(drawing by Wayne Giordano)

Matecumbe. The remaining native divers all bore Spanish first names, such as Andrés, Domingo, and Pedro, but no last names, possibly indicating they had not yet been baptized.

Delayed by bad weather, Melgar did not locate the wreck site until June and because of continued foul weather, swift currents, and dangerous shoals, was only able to put divers down for a few days. The ballast pile was forty-three feet deep, and only some of the divers could reach it. Nevertheless, the expedition recovered twenty-five large silver bars, seven small bars, numerous silver plates, and other silver items. Needing to replenish their supply of fresh water, Melgar sailed for a nearby key. On the way, he encountered two English sloops manned with a combined total of thirty men. After a brief exchange of gunfire, Melgar decided to break off the engagement and return to Havana in order to save the treasure he had already recovered.

In May of the following year, Melgar set out from Havana to resume salvage operations on the *Maravillas*. Once again, with just two Spanish divers aboard, he first sailed to the Keys to get native divers. At Key West, his Spanish divers recovered some cannon from the wreck of a Dutch ship, and he was able to persuade two natives, one a diver, to come with him. Continuing up the Keys, he recruited eleven more divers at various native villages, including ones on Bahia Honda and Key Vaca. At one of the Matecumbe Keys, he found an English vessel with a crew of five Englishmen and two Negroes which had gone aground. Manning her with a prize crew, he sent her back to Havana with, amazingly, an Indian serving as pilot.

On arriving at the site, four natives, searching from a dugout, quickly located the wreck, and diving began. In just three and a half days, the divers recovered 2,975 pounds of silver. They also recovered many pieces of silverware, such as plates and basins, as well as hundreds of coins. Melgar discovered that the natives were concealing coins in their breeches but was reluctant to make an issue of it for fear they would stop work. In the end, he allowed the natives to keep 1,248 badly-corroded coins as payment for their efforts which, he said, were the "principal instruments" of recovering the silver. On the advice of his pilot, Melgar stopped operations on the fourth day and departed because of the dangerous nature of the site and the fear that the weather would deteriorate. On his way back to Havana, he stopped in the Keys to return the divers to their native villages.

During another Spanish salvage expedition in the vicinity of the Marquesas Keys in 1678, some native divers decided they would rather hunt turtles than treasure. After a turtle sounded, one of the natives dove in and speared it. As he neared the bottom, he sighted a pile of ballast from a shipwreck, but it did not prove to be the *Atocha*. During the same salvage operation, the leader found that he had to have a Spanish diver check on the natives; otherwise they would go down and come right up, saying "Nothing is there."

When some Spanish ships were lost on the coast of Cuba in 1698, the governor of Havana persuaded native divers from Key Largo and the Marquesas Keys to work on the wrecks. In return for their efforts, he promised them rum worth 2,660 pesos, as well as tobacco, baize cloth, and other trinkets.

The last major Spanish salvage operation in the Keys was the recovery of treasure from the galleons wrecked in the hurricane of 1733. In July of that year, a twenty-two-ship convoy returning to Spain was struck by a hurricane two days after leaving Havana. Fifteen ships were driven ashore or sunk between Key Vaca and Elliott Key. Most of the passengers and crewmen made it to shore by paddling boats or rafts or by swimming, but three large ships sank with the loss of several hundred lives.

The survivors began work to recover treasure within days after they were cast ashore. Soon after news of the disaster reached Havana, the Spanish established fortified salvage camps on the Keys near the wrecks and employed native divers to assist in underwater recovery of treasure. When a ship could not be refloated, the salvors burned it to the waterline in order to allow the divers easier access to the cargo hold. Salvage efforts continued for several years, and while most of the treasure was saved, there was still plenty left for modern treasure hunters.

As a result of white men's guns, diseases, and rum, as well as slave raids by bands of Native Americans from territory north of Florida, most of the original natives of the Keys were gone by the middle of the eighteenth century. The departing Spanish took the few remaining survivors to Cuba when they relinquished Florida to the English in 1763.

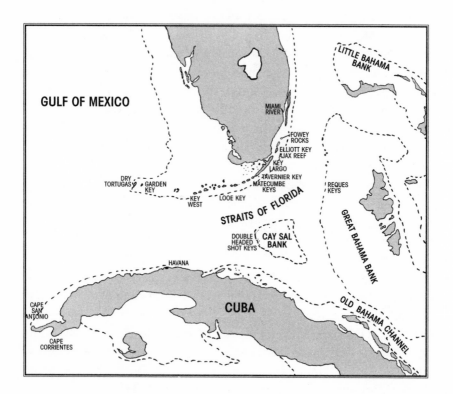

Chapter 2

CASTAWAYS

*T*he combination of hidden reefs, unpredictable currents, and powerful storms, coupled with mariners' primitive navigational instruments and inaccurate charts, took a terrible toll on ships and crews transiting the Straits of Florida in the sixteenth, seventeenth, and eighteenth centuries. Survivors of shipwrecks on the Florida Reef in those times were not much better off than those who drowned. Their chances of rescue by a passing ship were slim. If they did not die of thirst or starvation, there was a good possibility the Keys natives would find them and kill or enslave them. If a Spanish ship discovered the castaways, and they were English or other enemies of Spain, they might be imprisoned or hanged in Havana. Most of the stories of the unfortunate mariners who were cast up on the Florida Reef and Keys have disappeared with them, but a few tales of their misfortunes have survived.

Encounters with the Natives
By the mid-1500s, the Keys natives had lost any of the fear or awe of Europeans they once might have felt. Some authorities believe that Spanish

Shipwreck survivors on the Florida Reef faced death or enslavement at the hands of Keys natives or death from starvation and thirst on deserted Keys (*Harper's Weekly*, Vol. 1, No. 40, October 3, 1857. From the collections of The Mariners' Museum, Newport News, Virginia)

slave traders from Puerto Rico had been carrying off natives from Florida even before Ponce de León planted the Spanish flag there in 1513. If true, it adds one more explanation for the hostility of the natives to European intruders.

The earliest record of a castaway in the Keys is found in the account of Hernando D'Escalante Fontaneda. In 1549, at age thirteen, Fontaneda was on his way from Cartagena to Spain to be educated when the ship he was on wrecked in the Keys. The natives captured the survivors and enslaved them. Fontaneda spent seventeen years in captivity among various Florida tribes, eventually becoming a prisoner of the Calusa, a powerful and warlike tribe that lived on the west coast in the vicinity of Charlotte Harbor. The Calusa exercised dominion over the Florida Keys and forced the Keys natives to hand over any captives and treasure they obtained from ship-wrecks as tribute.

In 1566, Pedro Menéndez de Avilés, founder of St. Augustine and first governor of Florida, sailed around the Keys to explore the southwest coast of Florida and to meet the chief of the Calusa. He was also searching for his son, who had been lost somewhere along the coast. At the principal village of the Calusa, he found and rescued Fontaneda and seventeen other ship-wreck survivors who had been slaves of the Calusa for many years. Many of the survivors' companions, including Fontaneda's brother, had been killed in annual sacrificial ceremonies.

The Spanish made a number of attempts to pacify and Christianize the natives of South Florida and the Keys, including establishing missions at the principal villages of the Calusa and the Tequesta (a tribe centered at the mouth of the Miami River). Their efforts were less than successful. In 1571, a small sailboat on its way from St. Augustine to Havana stopped at the Matecumbe Keys to fish. Onboard were nine soldiers. They felt safe stop-ping there because the chief of the Matecumbe natives was supposedly at peace with the Spanish and had allowed his son to be taken to Havana to be educated as a Christian. A band of natives met the soldiers, told them that they were friends of Governor Menéndez, and invited them into their huts. They gave the soldiers fish to eat and water to drink, but when the soldiers were relaxed, they attacked them with clubs and spears. Only one soldier, Andrés Calderón, although wounded, survived. He remained a cap-tive until he was ransomed by Menéndez twenty months later. Oddly, Calderón reported that during his captivity he was fed by an Indian whom he described as his friend.

This incident and other murders of castaways in the Keys and else-where on the coast of Florida brought Menéndez to the end of his patience. In 1573, he petitioned the King of Spain to allow him to either kill or enslave all the coastal natives who were a menace to shipwrecked seamen. The king denied the request. Four years later, in 1577, when two Spanish vessels from Havana wrecked at the head of the Keys, the natives killed all the survivors except two they held for ransom. The following year, in the same location, the natives showed more mercy. After killing four or five shipwrecked Spaniards, they held the remaining thirty for ransom.

Apparently, the Keys natives were beginning to realize that they had more to gain by keeping their captives alive. When Menéndez' successor, Pedro Menéndez Marqués, voyaged down the coast as far as the Keys in 1580 looking for two Spanish captives, he found that the natives were more inclined to peace. He warned them that he would punish them if they killed any more castaways. The natives agreed they would not, and Marqués promised he would ransom any Christians who fell into their hands.

So far as can be determined from available records, the Keys natives did not kill Spanish castaways after 1600. In fact, when the Spanish frigate *Nuestra Señora del Rosario* ran aground off the Matecumbe Keys in 1605, the natives came out in their dugouts and said they were friends of the Spanish and had visited St. Augustine. The frigate remained aground for two or three days. The natives provided the stranded crew and passengers with fish, fresh water, and firewood, and even helped in freeing the vessel. Amazingly, they returned intact all the items brought ashore to lighten the ship.

Although the Spanish promised to ransom any Christian castaways, that promise did not include their enemies, the English. In fact, as the years went by with more frequent contacts between the natives and Spanish fishermen from Cuba, the natives gradually absorbed the Spanish hatred of the English. The governor of Cuba wrote the King of Spain in 1743 arguing against a plan to bring the Keys natives to Cuba to be converted to the Catholic faith. Instead, he said, they should be kept in the Keys and missionaries sent to them to save their souls. This, he said, would "build a colony of friends in a place of great importance where, even while remaining savages, they have contributed many times to the saving of shipwrecked Spaniards and as a scourge for the enemy [the English]." The governor went on to cite several instances in which the Keys natives had attacked and killed the crews of English vessels passing by the Keys.

Following the governor's recommendation, two Jesuit fathers and a dozen soldiers were sent to establish a mission in the Keys. But, upon arriving there, they learned that all the Keys natives had moved to a village at the mouth of the Miami River. At the village they found approximately one hundred men, women, and children including remnants of the Keys, Calusa, and Bocaratones tribes. The group was migratory, dividing its time among the Miami River, keys in Florida Bay, Key Vaca, and areas along the southwest coast.

The natives gave the priests a rude reception, denying that they had ever asked for missionaries. It soon became apparent that without a stronger force of soldiers to protect the mission and to stop the natives from running away, there was no hope of converting them. Two months after its inception, the mission was abandoned.

The following story takes place five years later, in 1748, while England and Spain were still at war. It demonstrates that the hatred of the English that the Spanish had aroused in the natives of south Florida was still alive.

The Miraculous Deliverance of Britton Hammon

A Massachusetts sloop, homeward bound from the Caribbean with a cargo of logwood, struck the Florida Reef in June 1748. Among the crewmen was a slave named Britton Hammon who had shipped aboard some six months earlier at Plymouth, Massachusetts, with the permission of his master. The narrative that follows is taken from Hammon's own account of his incredible experiences during the nearly thirteen years that followed the shipwreck.

Based on Hammon's sparse description ("on Cape Florida about five leagues from shore"), the sloop might have wrecked on Fowey Rocks, about halfway between the head of the Keys and Key Biscayne. After two days of fruitless efforts to haul the ship off with a line to an anchor, the crew begged the captain to throw part of the cargo of logwood overboard to lighten the ship. The captain refused and instead ordered the sloop's boat launched with the intention of moving ashore and setting up camp until help arrived.

Crewmen loaded the boat with arms, ammunition, provisions, and sails to make tents. The mate and eight seamen, including Hammon, boarded for the first trip to shore, leaving the captain and two others onboard to await the boat's return.

When they were about halfway to shore, the landing party sighted a large number of dugout canoes headed toward them. Their spirits soared when they saw the English colors displayed in one of the canoes, but then sank a short while later when they realized the paddlers were Native Americans, not Englishmen. By this time, the canoes were so close there was no possibility of escape.

Twenty canoes manned by some sixty natives armed with muskets surrounded the boat. Several of them jumped aboard the boat and seized the arms, ammunition, and provisions. Leaving two canoes to escort the boat, the rest of the band paddled rapidly toward the wrecked sloop. The natives in the two remaining canoes, signaling to the boat's crew to follow them, also headed for the sloop.

By the time the boat reached the wreck, the advance party of natives had already boarded and killed the captain and two seamen. As the boat drew closer, the crewmen saw the natives on deck reload their muskets. The mate cried out, "My lads, we are all dead men." Moments later, the warriors took aim and fired, killing three of the men in the boat. Preferring to drown rather than be shot, Hammon threw himself overboard. A few minutes later, he heard another volley of gunfire which, he later learned, dispatched all his remaining shipmates.

The natives in one of the canoes paddled after Hammon, hauled him aboard, beat him mercilessly with a cutlass, and then tied him up. Having plundered the sloop of everything they wanted, the natives set it on fire, howling and yelling as the flames leaped into the rigging.

When the wreck had burned to the water's edge, the entire party headed for shore, taking the sloop's boat and Hammon with them. On the way, in broken English, they told Hammon they were going to roast him alive.

The natives in one of the canoes hauled Hammon aboard and beat him mercilessly with a cutlass (drawing by Wayne Giordano)

When they reached the shore, they led the black man to one of their huts. Hammon was certain he was about to die. Instead, after a time, they untied him and fed him boiled corn. They kept him under guard but did not further mistreat him. From their long association with the Spanish, the natives knew the value of slaves and had probably decided to hold him for ransom.

Five weeks later, a Spanish schooner arrived to trade with the natives, and Hammon's hopes rose. In the first of two amazing coincidences, Hammon recognized the captain as a man named Romond, whom he had met in Jamaica when the sloop had stopped there. Romond had been brought to Jamaica as a prisoner after his ship had been captured by an English privateer. Having been in a similar situation himself, the captain was sympathetic to Hammon's plight. He asked the natives to allow Hammon to come aboard his vessel, which they did. As soon as Hammon was aboard, the captain weighed anchor and sailed for Havana.

Infuriated by the loss of their valuable captive, the natives determined to retrieve him. Just four days after the schooner moored at Havana, the natives arrived and demanded the return of their prisoner. Whether they came in their own dugout canoes or aboard a Cuban fishing boat, Hammon does not say. When the captain refused to release Hammon, the natives obtained an audience with the governor of Havana and repeated their demand for Hammon's return. The governor, briefed on the events at the wreck, told the natives that he would not release Hammon to them because they had murdered the entire crew of the English ship. But, to maintain friendly relations, he gave them ten dollars as payment for Hammon. Probably because the war with England was drawing to a close, he warned them not to kill any more castaways, but to take them captive and bring them to Havana, where he would pay ten dollars a head for them.

The rest of Hammon's story is as incredible as its beginning. For about a year, he was kept working at the governor's mansion as a servant. One day as he was walking in the city, a Spanish navy press gang seized him. When he refused to serve in the navy, he was thrown into jail, which he described as a "close dungeon." He remained there for four years and seven months. Finally, through the intervention of a merchant ship captain from Boston and an English woman who took pity on his situation, he was released but forced to return to the service of the governor.

Two years later, Hammon managed to escape aboard an English man-of-war. He served on several Royal Navy ships until he was severely wounded in a battle in which seventy of his shipmates were killed. Disabled for further naval service, he found employment as a cook aboard a merchant ship but then became seriously ill. When he recovered, he was destitute. In a London tavern, he heard of a ship being made ready for a voyage to New England and signed on as cook. After coming aboard, he overheard someone mention the name Winslow, the name of his former master. In the second remarkable coincidence of his adventures, it proved that a passenger onboard was, in fact, his former "good Master." Having long since given Hammon up for dead, Winslow was overjoyed to find him alive.

In Hammon's own words, "and tho' I have omitted a great many Things, yet what is wrote may suffice to convince the Reader, that I have been most grievously afflicted, an yet thro' the Divine Goodness, as miraculously preserved, and delivered out of many Dangers; of which I desire to retain a grateful Remembrance, as long as I live in the World."

British Men-of-War on the Reef

As a result of unwarranted harassment of British merchant shipping in the Caribbean by Spanish *guarda-costas* (privately owned coast guard vessels), England declared war against Spain in 1739, and hostilities continued until 1748.

The Spanish government had long prohibited foreign nations from trading with its American colonies except under very restricted circumstances. The prohibition was largely ignored by British merchant traders and Spanish colonials. The Spanish authorities delegated enforcement of the trading prohibition to the *guarda-costas*. Only one step above pirates, the *guarda-costas* stopped and seized British vessels, often without cause, and sometimes brutalized and even murdered their crews.

The war was known as the War of Jenkins' Ear because of an incident that took place in 1731. A *guarda-costa* vessel stopped and boarded a British merchant ship whose captain's name was Robert Jenkins. The *guarda-costa's* crew tortured Jenkins to find out where he had hidden his money by alternately hanging him and then cutting him down before he died. In the end, they spared his life but cut off his ear. Supposedly, when Jenkins told his story and displayed his withered ear before Parliament, the ministry was forced by popular outrage to declare war against Spain.

During the war, British and Spanish warships and privateers frequently transited the Straits of Florida on their way to and from operations in the Caribbean, in the Gulf of Mexico, and along the North American East Coast. The dangers of navigation in the Straits were amply demonstrated during the conflict. The British lost one ship-of-the-line and two frigates, and the Spanish also lost a ship-of-the-line. None of these losses resulted from enemy action. Two hazardous coral reefs along the Florida Keys still bear the names of British frigates lost during the War of Jenkins' Ear.

In the last year of the war, 1748, the forty-four-gun frigate HMS *Fowey,* with a crew of two hundred men and a captured Spanish ship in tow, was escorting a merchant ship convoy northward through the Straits of Florida. She sighted one of the tiny islands of Cay Sal Bank and set a course based on that sighting. Unfortunately, the charts of those days were very unreliable. The *Fowey* and the Spanish prize, as well as one of the merchant ships,

Two British frigates, HMS *Fowey* and HMS *Loo,* were lost on the Florida
Reef during the War of Jenkins' Ear and left their names there: Fowey
Rocks and Looe Key (from an illustration in *Harper's Weekly,* February 10, 1838.
From the collections of The Mariners' Museum, Newport News, Virginia)

grounded on a reef near the head of the Keys. Although the crew was able, after strenuous efforts, to kedge the frigate off the rocks, she leaked so much that she had to be abandoned. The crew then transferred to two of the merchant ships, one of which had the misfortune to be captured later by a Spanish privateer.

According to the noon sight taken by one of the *Fowey's* officers, she grounded off Elliott Key on Ajax Reef, which was later confirmed by a 1996 archaeological survey. Her name, however, is forever attached to a rocky area eleven miles further north, now called Fowey Rocks.

A much more serious situation presented itself to the crew of a British frigate when, on the night of February 4, 1744, their ship ran aground on the Florida Reef and began to sink among the coral heads.

HMS Loo Bestows Her Name on a Key

On the day before striking the Florida reef, the forty-gun British frigate HMS *Loo,* commanded by Capt. Ashby Utting, had captured a former British merchant ship, manned by a Spanish crew, in the Straits of Florida. With the merchantman in tow, Captain Utting took departure from a position twenty miles north of Matanzas Bay, Cuba, on course northeast by north. His main navigational concern was to avoid the Double Headed Shot Cays (part of Cay Sal Bank) on the eastern side of the Straits. At midnight, believing he was well clear of this hazard, he ordered the course changed to northeast and went below to his cabin.

An hour later, as the watch on deck was preparing to take the regular half-hourly sounding with the deep-sea lead line, the officer on watch saw breakers ahead. He immediately ordered the helmsman to put the rudder hard over and called the captain. By the time Utting arrived on deck, the ship's bow was into the wind and it appeared she would turn clear of the breakers. But before the frigate gained headway on the opposite tack, the stern struck, and in rapid succession, the tiller snapped, the rudder broke, and water started flooding into the hold.

The captain ordered the boats swung out and the pumps manned. Just as the men at the pumps were beginning to make headway against the inrushing water, a series of large swells threw the frigate violently against the coral heads and stove in the bottom planks. The ship began to sink rapidly. Realizing there was no hope of saving his ship, Utting ordered the sailing master to save the bread and the gunner to save gunpowder.

Moments after the *Loo* struck the reef, her prize struck also. The swells rolled the merchantman over on her side. Seeing this, Utting shouted an order to the prize crew to cut away her masts and jettison the cannon and anchors. When this was done, the merchant ship righted herself and lay more quietly but continued to settle deeper in the water.

Now it was evident that there was no hope of saving either vessel. In the dim light of early morning, the captain could see the faint shape of a small sand spit showing above the water inside the breakers. He ordered the frigate's boats to carry the crew to the island.

Until dawn, Utting believed he had struck the Double Headed Shot Cays, but when he saw the low-lying, dark green line of islands two miles to the north, he realized he was on the reef of the Martyrs (as the Florida Keys were then called). The tiny island on which his crew had taken refuge no longer exists, but the coral heads which sank his ship are still there, known today as Looe Key.

The situation of the 274 men comprising the crew of the frigate and their Spanish prisoners was a desperate one. They were cast away in enemy territory with only enough food and water to last a few days. Their island was only about three hundred yards long, a hundred wide, and not more than a foot above water. The smallest storm would wash them off their precarious perch. If they were not discovered and captured by the Spanish, they were likely to be massacred by the Keys natives. Their only means of escape were the frigate's three boats, which could not carry more than a third of their number.

At mid-morning, their salvation appeared in the form of a small sloop approaching from offshore, but when they signaled to it, the sloop bore away. Utting immediately ordered the boats to be manned with armed seamen and marines and directed his officers to pursue and capture the sloop without fail.

As the sloop disappeared over the horizon, with the ships' boats in pursuit, crewmen set to work cutting holes in the frigate's decks to gain access to her stores of water and provisions. By the end of the day, they had managed to salvage only two water casks. As night fell with no sign of the boats, the captain posted twenty-five marines and twenty-five seamen around the periphery of the island to guard against an Indian attack.

The next morning brought the welcome sight of the boats returning in company with the sloop. Her Spanish crew had abandoned her and were unquestionably on their way to Havana in a small boat to inform the Spanish naval authorities of the presence of a wrecked British warship in the Keys. Fearful of an imminent attack by the Indians or a Spanish warship, some of the crew became rebellious, growling amongst themselves and clamoring to leave the island immediately. Utting decided the best policy was to ignore them and, with those who were willing to work, renewed the task of getting water and provisions out of the frigate. Preparing the boats for sea, extracting more stores from the frigate, and loading the sloop and the boats continued all the next day. The longboat's capacity and seaworthiness were improved by adding a plank above the gunwale, thereby increasing its freeboard.

Four days after striking the reef, the *Loo*'s officers and men had completed preparations for departure and had embarked in the boats: 184 in the sloop, 60 in the longboat, 20 in the barge, and 10 in the yawl. While the other boats stood by at a safe distance, the captain, the gunner, and the barge crew went aboard the *Loo* and placed gunpowder kegs and combustible materials along the starboard gun deck, which was still partly out of water. After setting the materials afire, they rowed off and stayed until nightfall watching the ship burn and then finally explode. Utting was still concerned that the Spanish would recover some of the *Loo*'s guns and anchors.

The heavily overloaded sloop and boats set sail for New Providence Island in the Bahamas, but the boats quickly outsailed the sloop. By midnight, the captain, now onboard the sloop, lost sight of them. The wind freshened and he became concerned that the overloaded sloop, with the wind abeam, would capsize. He tacked the sloop to head north and bring the wind astern. Although a northward course would take him along the enemy's coast and past their stronghold at St. Augustine, it was a lesser risk than capsizing and drowning.

The sloop passed St. Augustine without being sighted and reached

Port Royal, South Carolina, after five days of sailing. The barge made its way across the Great Bahama Bank and reached New Providence safely. The yawl, the smallest of the boats, encountered heavy seas and contrary winds and was driven southward to the coast of Cuba. Just as her crew had resigned themselves to a long internment in a Havana prison, a British frigate rescued them. No record of the longboat's voyage has been found, but inasmuch as one of her officers was present at the subsequent court-martial, it is apparent that she made a safe port. It was a miraculous escape for all hands.

Two months after the loss of his frigate, Captain Utting sailed to England to face a court-martial. In his testimony before the court, he cited his many years of experience in navigating the Straits of Florida and his conviction that he had steered a correct course. He was backed up by pilots familiar with the passage. The court agreed and attributed the loss of HMS *Loo* to an unusual change in the direction and speed of the Gulf Stream current.

The court exonerated Captain Utting and returned him to command of another frigate. But misfortune continued to hound him. Just two years after the loss of the *Loo*, he contracted a fever and died aboard his ship in Charleston harbor.

The third British man-of-war to be lost in the Keys during the War of Jenkins' Ear was the ship-of-the-line HMS *Tyger*. Of the three British Navy crews shipwrecked in the Keys during that conflict, none faced a more hopeless situation than did the crew of the *Tyger*. Their story, which follows, is derived from the captain's journal, the ship's log, and the records of court-martials of the ship's officers.

Cast Away on the Dry Tortugas—The Remarkable
Escape of the Crew of HMS Tyger

Post Capt. Edward Herbert, commanding HMS *Tyger*, fifty guns, paced his quarterdeck in frustration. England and Spain were again at war, and his orders were to capture or destroy any Spanish vessels encountered. After three weeks on station off the western tip of Cuba in December 1741, his only captures were three small native sailing craft called *periaguas*. From one of their crewmen he learned that a Spanish force was about to sail from Vera Cruz to Havana and that some ships at Havana were preparing to put to sea for Vera Cruz. Captain Herbert decided to keep the three *periaguas* rather than sink them. It was a decision which was to have fortunate consequences for everyone onboard.

For another week, the *Tyger* continued patrolling the same area while her captain, tormented by thoughts of the rich prizes that would soon pass by out of reach, struggled with the temptation to go after them. When three more days passed without sight of a sail, he decided to risk leaving his assigned station and move north into the Gulf of Mexico.

A fourth-rate ship-of-the-line, the *Tyger* had been rebuilt three times since her original launching in 1647. After the last rebuilding in 1722, she was 130 feet long and displaced 700 tons. She mounted 22 eighteen-pounder guns on the main deck, 22 nine-pounders on the upper deck, and 6 six-pounders on the quarterdeck. Her crew was comprised of 281 officers and men, 57 of whom were marines.

For the next week after leaving station, the *Tyger* sailed on generally northerly courses while the Florida Current carried her to the east. At 9:00

HMS *Tyger*, 50-gun, fourth-rate ship-of-the-line lost at the Dry Tortugas, January 1742
(courtesy of Mr. R. J. G. Berkeley, Berkeley Castle. Photograph by Courtland Institute of Art, London)

P.M. on January 11, the leadsman reported a sounding of thirty-five fathoms. Soundings continued to decrease throughout the night. Thinking he was approaching the western edge of the Bahama Bank, the captain ordered a course change to the south. In the morning, the masthead lookout sighted some small islands to the northwest. The master (warrant officer-navigator) and pilot agreed that the islands were probably the Tortugas (known today as the Dry Tortugas). Discovered by Ponce de León in 1513 and named for the many turtles found there, the Dry Tortugas are located seventy miles west of Key West in the Gulf of Mexico. The low-lying islands, devoid of any source of fresh water, lie in the midst of a large area of shoals and treacherous coral reefs.

At 1:00 P.M. on the day the islands were sighted, the *Tyger* chased and came up with a sloop manned by a prize crew from a Rhode Island privateer. The prize crew's captain said they had recaptured the sloop from the Spanish and were in desperate need of food and water. He also advised the crew of the *Tyger* that the islands they had sighted were not the Tortugas but the Reques Keys, which lie on the western edge of Great Bahama Bank nearly two hundred miles to the east of the Tortugas. Assuming the prize crew's knowledge of their position was better than his own, Captain Herbert accepted the information as correct.

The *Tyger's* boat crew transferred food and water to the sloop and brought back a Spanish prisoner the prize crew considered dangerous. By this time night had fallen, and soundings had gradually decreased to twenty-five fathoms. Thirty minutes after parting company with the sloop, the leadsman called out a depth of eight fathoms. The officer on watch immediately ordered the ship to be tacked, but she failed to complete the maneuver, fell off before the wind, and, moments later, struck bottom forward.

The captain, now on deck, ordered the sails backed, and the *Tyger* broke free. He then ordered the sails clewed up (so as to spill the wind) and the anchor let go. But the anchor was not ready, and before it could be cut away, the ship grounded again. This time all efforts to move the ship off with the sails proved futile. Rising winds and seas prevented carrying out an anchor until morning. In the meantime, as the ship pounded on the coral rocks, the water level in the hold began rising despite the best efforts of the crew working both pumps.

At 8:00 A.M., the winds and seas had abated sufficiently to permit the longboat crew to carry out an anchor. Seamen heaved around on the capstan to try to drag the ship off the rocks, but she would not move. By noon it was evident that the ship was lost and that the only remaining course of action was to take refuge on the nearest island, about a mile and a half distant. It was Garden Key.

The ship's boats began ferrying men, water, and provisions ashore. In addition to the three captured *periaguas,* the *Tyger* carried a longboat (heavy-duty sea boat, about thirty feet), a barge (officers' harbor boat, also about thirty feet), and a yawl (smaller sea boat, about twenty-three feet). All three ship's boats were equipped to be rowed or sailed. There was also a native canoe onboard, large enough to carry a dozen men.

On the second day, a rumor spread among the crew that since their ship was a wreck and they were on dry land, they were free to do as they pleased. The captain assembled the men and advised them that not only were they still subject to naval authority, they were also in a very serious predicament. There were not sufficient boats to carry them away, the provisions and water they could salvage from the wreck would last only a few weeks, and there was a very good chance that the Spanish would discover them and attack. Only by all hands working together toward a common goal, he said, was there any chance for their survival. The men indicated that they understood and were ready to do their part.

For the next few days, seamen continued to ferry water, provisions, and other supplies ashore and erect tents made from sails for sleeping quarters and storerooms. On January 18, six days after the wreck, the longboat, manned by a crew of eight under command of the master, departed for New Providence in the Bahamas to obtain help.

After most of the provisions and water casks that were not underwater had been brought ashore, the majority of the crew began working on the island's defenses. Onboard ship, the gunner directed operations to hoist the nine-pounder guns, each weighing a ton, over the side onto rafts to be ferried ashore. Onshore, the carpenters constructed gun platforms from planks torn up from the quarterdeck. Other men gathered tree branches and bushes and tied them together in large bundles called faschines. These were to be used to build defensive barriers. The remaining crewmen dug trenches in front of the battery sites.

The eighteen-pounder guns on the main deck, now sunk to water level, were useless where they were. The carpenters cut access openings in the upper deck, and with block and tackle—and the muscle power of one hundred seamen—remounted the four-thousand-pound monsters on the upper deck. The wrecked hulk of the *Tyger* was now part of the line of defense.

As the defensive works neared completion, the most pressing problem became the limited supply of food and water. After the first week onshore, Captain Herbert cut the crew's rations in half. Working from dawn to dusk under a blazing sun, the marooned crew began to feel the pinch of hunger and the ebbing of their strength. Onboard the *Tyger,* seamen dived down into the dark, flooded hold to fasten lines to provision and water casks so they could be hoisted out through openings cut in the main deck. Other crewmen daily manned boats that could be spared from ferrying operations and set out to shoot birds, gather shellfish, and catch fish, turtles, and monk seals.

When the crew had completed the defensive works, they had mounted all the nine-pounder and six-pounder guns, a total of twenty-eight, in batteries at strategic points around the island. A sketch made by a Spanish ship sometime after the *Tyger's* crew had escaped from the island shows the position of the wreck and the layout of the encampment and fortifications.

As days passed, concern for the fate of the longboat grew. When there was no news of her on February 6, nineteen days after her departure, the captain ordered the yawl prepared for another attempt to get help from the Bahamas. Two days later, the second lieutenant, Lieutenant Craig, and eight seamen sailed away to the east.

On February 16, only eight days after her departure, the yawl returned. Craig reported that they had sailed about one hundred miles when they came to a group of many low-lying islands which he was sure were the "islands on Cape Florida," today known as the Florida Keys. The captain now knew that the *Tyger* had, in fact, wrecked on the Tortugas.

The yawl's crew had seen Indians onshore and a Spanish schooner with several sloops nearby. One sloop had chased the yawl and fired at her. After barely escaping capture, Craig had decided to return to the Tortugas to report what he had seen to the captain. Captain Herbert immediately made plans to send a strong force in boats to attempt to capture one or more of the Spanish vessels. The following morning, fifty-five seamen and marines under the command of the first lieutenant, Lieutenant Farrish, along with Craig and Lieutenant Scott of the Royal Marines, sailed away "with a merry heart," as the captain recorded in his journal.

Recognizing the possibility that the expedition might not be successful,

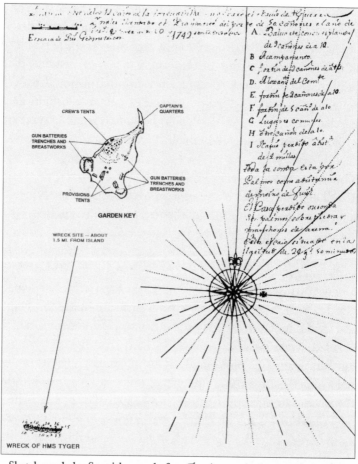

Sketch made by Spanish vessel after *Tyger's* crew had escaped showing HMS *Tyger* wreck site and fortifications and encampment on Garden Key
(from a document found in Biblioteca Nacional, Madrid, by treasure salvor Jack Haskins)

the captain ordered the carpenter to proceed with plans to enlarge the third *periagua*. The carpenter's crew hauled the boat ashore, cut her apart, and began lengthening her with lumber from the wreck.

The *Tyger's* crew had now been marooned on the Tortugas for over a month with no indication that the Spanish, only ninety miles away at Havana, were aware of their presence. But their hopes of remaining undiscovered came to an end on the morning of February 20, when they sighted a sail to the east. The vessel headed for the wreck where the third lieutenant, Lieutenant Dennis, and several men were working. As she came closer, Dennis saw that she was a Spanish half-galley with sixty to seventy armed men onboard. The lieutenant and his men made for shore while the Spanish galley moored alongside the wreck.

All hands prepared to repel an attack, but in the morning they saw that the Spanish crewmen were busily engaged in replacing their mainmast with two topmasts taken from the *Tyger*. With only two small boats available, the canoe and the yawl, Captain Herbert reluctantly concluded that an attempt to take the galley was not possible. The next morning, her new mast in place, the galley sailed away.

Now that their situation was known to the Spanish, the captain realized that they could expect an attack at any time. He directed the officers to remove from the *Tyger* anything of value to the enemy and to prepare the wreck to be set on fire at a moment's notice. These preparations were made none too soon. Two days later, another sail was sighted approaching from the northeast. She proved to be a large sloop. When the sloop, with English colors flying, had anchored about a mile from the wreck and out of range of the shore batteries, she launched a boat which headed toward the wreck. Dennis, again onboard the *Tyger*, suspected that the sloop was Spanish. When he saw that the boat was filled with armed men, he set fire to the wreck and headed for shore.

Captain Herbert, also thinking the English colors were a ruse, sent a boat to investigate. In English, a man on the sloop invited the boat's crew to come aboard, but fearing trickery, they declined and returned to report to the captain. The captain then sent Dennis out in the canoe with a flag of truce. A boat from the sloop, also flying a white flag, advanced to meet him.

One of the men in the sloop's boat, speaking in English, admitted that the sloop's crew were Spanish. He informed Dennis that the *Tyger's* longboat had been captured by Keys natives, who had killed three of its crew and turned the rest over to a Spanish ship. The captured men were now in prison at Havana. The Spanish spokesman asked how the *Tyger's* crew were faring on the island and offered to furnish food and water. Stiffly, Dennis thanked the Spaniard and said they had no need of help. The boats then parted. The *Tyger's* men stood by their guns through the night, but at dawn the sloop was gone. In the meantime, the wreck burned to the waterline.

Shortly after dark the following evening, the first boat of the expedition to the Keys returned. It was the barge with Scott in command. The marine officer reported that, after reaching the Keys, they had found an abandoned sloop which had been badly damaged in a gun battle. It was the same sloop the *Tyger* had aided shortly before running aground. Apparently, the Spanish had recaptured it and then abandoned it because of the damage. The first lieutenant and a party of men had made temporary repairs to the sloop's hull, had jury-rigged a sail using the men's jackets and trousers, and were on their way back to the Tortugas.

Because of her limited sailing abilities, the reclaimed sloop did not reach the island until the afternoon after the barge arrived. Upon dropping anchor, Farrish fired a seven-gun salute to Captain Herbert. A five-gun salute was returned from shore to the resourceful lieutenant who had brought back the means of their escape from the island.

A little more than six weeks had now passed. While the rations of water, rum, and food had steadily decreased, the work had not. With the time for departure near, the pace increased. The men could not help but notice fifteen casks of rum and fifteen casks of water being brought ashore from the captured sloop. They fully expected that their rum and water rations would be increased. When it was not, they began to grumble among themselves. Their discontent was further aggravated by observing that the captain and his servants, as well as his chickens, hogs, and sheep, always had a plentiful supply of food and water.

A few bold seamen went to the captain's tent to request an increase in their grog and water rations. Suspecting what they had come for, the captain swore that he would "by God, blow the brains out of the first man who offered to speak, grumble, or ask for more rum and water." Frustrated by the captain's threat, the men asked Scott to intercede for them. The marine lieutenant was young, inexperienced, and sympathetic to the crew's hardships. Concerned that the men might take more drastic action, he agreed to draw up a petition to the captain on their behalf.

The next afternoon, Scott and a large number of the crew assembled in front of the captain's tent. Scott requested permission to speak to the captain. When the captain emerged from his tent, the lieutenant asked the men if he spoke for them. They replied "Aye, aye," and he began reading the petition. In Scott's words, the crew complained about the short rations of water and food considering that there was more in storage than could be carried off when they left. They asked if it was "not monstrous cruelty in you [the captain] to inflict such hardships and miserys [sic] on us, your fellow creatures, who cannot have deserved such barbarous treatment. . . ." They also accused the captain of "a certain dilatoryness [sic] that inclines them to believe that you have no great inclination soon to leave this island." Finally, swearing they had no mutinous intent, they humbly begged to know whether or not they were asking for more than was their due.

After Scott had finished reading, Herbert asked him, "Who is in command?" When Scott replied, "You, sir," the captain ordered him to be placed under arrest and confined. Then, addressing the crew, the captain explained that although there were more provisions, water, and rum than they could take with them, he could not ignore the possibility that they might be besieged by the Spanish before they could get away. He then read the Articles of War, warned the crew against any further such conduct, and urged them to exert themselves so as to be able to leave the island as soon as possible. The next day, the captain increased the crew's water ration by a pint a day, and the men redoubled their efforts to complete repairing and rerigging the sloop and rebuilding the *periagua*.

On the afternoon of March 7, a vessel anchored about five miles off the island. The next morning, Farrish went out in the barge to investigate and found that it was the same large Spanish sloop that had visited them ten days earlier.

Although they knew that the sloop had a large crew and was armed with fourteen carriage guns and many swivel guns, the captain and his officers thought there was a reasonable chance of capturing her. They planned an attack using all available boats with the maximum number of men they could carry. Farrish, in the barge with nineteen men, would lead the attack force, supported by Craig in a *periagua* with nineteen men, Dennis in the larger *periagua* with twenty-seven men, Midshipman Moore in the yawl with fifteen men, and Midshipman Read in the canoe with eleven men.

The combined force of ninety-six officers and men rowed away from the island that evening and reached the vicinity of the sloop shortly after dark. As the boats moved to their assigned positions, a Spanish lookout sighted one of them and cried out an alarm. The men in the barge and the canoe gave three cheers, the agreed signal to attack, and rowed in to board the sloop's stern. As they approached, the Spanish crew began firing at them. Some of the men in Dennis' boat would not row and crouched down to avoid the enemy's fire.

Shouting to Dennis to "Come up, for God's sake," Farrish and his men climbed onboard over the port quarter while Read led the men in the canoe up over the starboard quarter. Dennis threatened to run his men through with his sword if they did not pull on their oars, but his words had little effect. In desperation, he and a midshipman each took an oar and began rowing. As they neared the sloop's stern, some of Dennis' men started firing and throwing grenades wildly. Their poorly aimed shots wounded sev-

One of the hastily thrown grenades landed in the barge and blew a hole in the bottom, sinking the barge (drawing by Wayne Giordano)

eral *Tyger* men onboard the sloop, including Farrish. With that setback, the tide of battle turned, and the boarding party began retreating to their boats.

At this critical point, one of the hastily thrown grenades landed in the barge and blew a hole in the bottom, causing it to sink. The crews of the canoe and the *periagua* rescued the barge crew from the water. As Farrish was pulled aboard the canoe, he was heard to call Dennis "a murdering dog" who had ruined him.

Farrish had ordered Craig and Moore to launch their attack at the sloop's bow. Claiming afterwards that they had not heard the three-cheers signal to attack, Craig and Moore did not reach the bow until five minutes after the attack at the stern had begun. Both boat crews boarded and began fighting at close quarters. As the fight at the bow began, the boarding party at the stern had started to retreat. The Spaniards wounded twelve of the forward boarding party, including Craig, who became weak from loss of blood. With their leader incapacitated, the *Tyger's* men lost spirit and withdrew to their boats. At this point, a breeze sprang up, the Spanish crew hoisted a jib and cut the anchor cable, and the sloop glided away from the *Tyger's* boats. The weary, dispirited crews rowed slowly back to the encampment. Although a number were wounded, none were killed.

Ten days later, preparations to leave the island were complete. The carpenters and sailmakers had repaired and rerigged the sloop. Other seamen had careened the sloop and scraped her underwater hull. The gunners had armed her with two nine-pounders, six six-pounders, and four swivel guns. The carpenters had also completed and launched the enlarged *periagua,* and the sailmakers had rerigged her as a two-masted schooner. The gunner's men broke off parts of all the remaining guns to render them useless to the enemy, and threw all shot and ironwork of any nature into deep water. After the boats were loaded, everything of value left on the island, including remaining provisions and gun powder, was set on fire.

At dawn on March 19, the officers and men of the *Tyger* boarded their assigned craft for the return to Jamaica. Approximately 180 men were onboard the sloop, 60 on the schooner-rigged *periagua,* and about 30 in the four small craft (yawl, two *periaguas,* and canoe). The feelings of relief and joy in the men's hearts as they sailed away from the desolate Tortugas after sixty-six days of unremitting toil, hunger, thirst, and fear can only be imagined.

The *Tyger's* boats were loaded far beyond their normal capacities (*Chronicles of the Sea* Vol. I, No. 90, 1838. From the collections of The Mariners' Museum, Newport News, Virginia)

The sloop and the boats were loaded far beyond their normal capacities. Ahead of them lay a voyage of seven hundred miles, much of it through enemy waters and with only a limited supply of food and water. The schooner and small craft could not keep up with the sloop and so were usually towed. On the second day, the canoe capsized and sank, but one of the other boats saved its crew. Making good progress to the southwest, the little flotilla rounded Cape San Antonio at the western tip of Cuba in just six days. There, a fresh gale forced them to seek shelter in Cape Corrientes Bay (thirty miles east of Cape San Antonio) for two days.

Five days after leaving Cape Corrientes, Grand Cayman Island came into view. But now, with the western tip of Jamaica only two hundred miles away, progress stopped. For three weeks, there were either no winds, head winds, or contrary currents. Living in cramped quarters with little food and less water, the men's tempers grew short. The captain recorded that Craig had behaved with "insolence and disobedience," and he ordered Dennis to relieve Craig of command of the schooner.

When the sloop was towing the schooner in moderate to strong winds, the sloop's speed was greatly reduced. In light winds, the schooner could outsail the sloop. Herbert concluded that each boat could make better progress on its own. He ordered Dennis to take the schooner north to the string of small keys that parallel the southern coast of Cuba and then make his way in protected waters to Cape Cruz at the southwestern tip of the island. The sloop and small craft would proceed on a direct course and rendezvous with him there. Failing that, Dennis was to proceed independently to the naval base at Port Royal, Jamaica. (There is no record of the schooner's subsequent voyage beyond the fact that her crew eventually reached Port Royal.)

Six days later, the sloop and small craft, having failed to rendezvous with Dennis, sailed into Lucey Bay at the western end of Jamaica. Their food and water were almost gone. From local plantations they obtained water, beef, bread, and yams. Beset by gales and broken gear, another three weeks passed before the boats reached Port Royal. In all, the voyage had taken fifty-six days.

Immediately on arrival, Herbert addressed a letter to Vice Admiral Edward Vernon charging Lieutenants Dennis and Craig with failure to press home the attack against the Spanish sloop and Lieutenant Scott with incitement to mutiny.

A little more than four months had passed since HMS *Tyger* had come to grief on the reefs of the Tortugas. Amazingly, in all that time, apart from the three crewmen in the longboat who had been killed by the Keys natives, only two seamen had died, both of natural causes. The long ordeal was over for the crew, but for *Tyger*'s officers, another was waiting.

Vice Admiral Vernon convened a court-martial at Port Royal on July

10, 1742, and directed the court to try the officers on the following charges: Capt. Edward Herbert for loss of HMS *Tyger;* Lieutenants Craig and Dennis for remissness in duty during the attack against a Spanish sloop; and Lieutenant Scott for mutinous behavior.

In deliberating the charges against Craig and Dennis, the court heard testimony from several crewmen who were in their boats during the attack. These men testified that the lieutenants had done everything in their power to lead their men into the fight. The *Tyger's* surgeon confirmed that Craig had, in fact, been severely wounded. Testimony was also produced that Farrish had selected the best men for his boat, leaving the least reliable men to go with Dennis, and these were men Dennis did not know well. The court acquitted both officers of the charges.

In the case of Lieutenant Scott, the court's members considered his conduct to be the result of inexperience and imprudence rather than any mutinous intent. They sentenced him to a severe reprimand.

The court found Captain Herbert guilty of a manifest breach of his orders for leaving his assigned patrol station. The court also found him guilty of failing to exercise prudent seamanship in not ordering an anchor to be made ready to drop upon first coming into shoal waters and of losing his ship as a consequence.

Notwithstanding the seriousness of the charges of which he was found guilty, the court was extremely lenient with the captain, according to the standards of the times. He was sentenced to lose all pay due him while serving as captain of HMS *Tyger.* But, in consideration of his leadership in saving the crew from possible death or capture by the Spanish while cast away on the Tortugas and in bringing them back safely to Jamaica, the court voted to recommend his continued service in the Royal Navy.

Old Animosities Threaten Castaways' Chances of Rescue
After the end of the Seven Years' War (French and Indian War in North America) in 1763, Spain ceded Florida to Great Britain in exchange for the recovery of Havana, which the British had captured. The departing Spaniards took the few natives remaining in the Keys with them to Cuba. For the next fifty-six years, the Keys were devoid of any permanent settle-

ments but were certainly not deserted. Each year from August to March, fleets of Cuban fishermen came to the Keys and the southwest coast of Florida to fish and to salt and dry their catches onshore. But even before Florida was turned over to the British, Bahamian vessels had begun coming to the Keys to catch turtles, cut hardwood timber, and salvage wrecks.

For sailors shipwrecked on the reef, the presence of the Bahamian turtling-wrecking craft was a godsend. A British surveyor, George Gauld, who charted the Keys from 1773 to 1775, cautioned shipwrecked mariners against abandoning their vessels. In his "Observations on the Florida Kays, Reef, and Gulf with Directions for Sailing among the Kays," he wrote, "The little vessels from Providence are constantly plying about those small islands, especially after a storm; they make lawful prize of all such as have been thus deserted; but they give every kind of assistance to those who, faithfully attending to the interest of the owner, remain with their ships till they are relieved; and if we consider the activity with which the Wreckers always exert themselves, we must look upon them as a set of very useful men."

With the end of the Revolutionary War in 1783, Florida reverted to Spain, but the change in ownership did nothing to change the situation in the Keys. Cuban fishermen and Bahamian wreckers continued to ply the Keys in pursuit of their trades. A proposal by a Spanish official in 1790 to drive the Bahamians out of the Keys came to naught. In fact, the number of Bahamian vessels there continued to increase.

Many examples could be cited to prove the truth of Gauld's assertion that the Bahamian wreckers gave every assistance to shipwrecked mariners. The master of the English ship *Sophia Bailey,* driven ashore on Cape Florida in 1785, had this to say of the four Bahamian wreckers who aided him in getting afloat: "Capt. Bell and the rest of the Captains have behaved with the greatest civility; and I shall make it my business to report their friendly conduct to all the underwriters at Lloyd's Coffee-house. You will be pleased to reward them for their trouble." Such willingness to render aid to distressed vessels was the norm, but there were rare exceptions when greed and long-standing hatred of the Spanish manifested itself in the behavior of individual Bahamian wrecking captains.

In 1785, a Spanish vessel ran aground on the reef off Key Largo. The captain of the first Bahamian wrecker on the scene ignored the frantic signals of Spanish crewmen in a boat and proceeded directly to the wreck in order to be first onboard. The Spanish crew was subsequently rescued by another Bahamian wrecker. Although England and Spain were not then at war, the first Bahamian captain claimed he was entitled to the entire amount of cargo he salvaged because the Spanish were enemies. When two Spanish mail ships wrecked off Key Largo in 1794, Bahamian wreckers plundered the ships while the crews were still onboard and demanded an exorbitant fee to carry the crews back to Havana. If it was not paid in cash, they threatened to leave the crews to their fates. The Spaniards had no choice but to pay.

The Bahamians' dislike and distrust of the Spanish was not entirely without basis and, as the following story illustrates, almost cost the lives of eleven castaway Americans.

A Narrow Escape at Key Largo

The following story comes from the memoirs of Vincent Nolte, a prominent merchant of the late 1700s and early 1800s. Widely traveled, his life was filled with so many interesting people and adventures that author Hervey Allen used him as one of the principal characters in his 1930s' best-selling novel, *Anthony Adverse*.

In January 1808, Nolte departed Havana aboard the schooner *Merchant* bound for Charleston through the Straits of Florida. At that time, Florida was still Spanish territory. For a day and a half, the schooner fought its way northeastward through gale-force winds. At 11:00 on the second night, she struck the Florida Reef. Nolte awoke with a start as a violent blow shook the whole ship and nearly threw him from his bunk. As he struggled into his clothes, he called to his black manservant and a traveling companion to follow him up on deck.

The night was black and the onrushing waves, driven by the howling gale, broke across the deck. The captain, still befuddled from a heavy drinking session before turning in, staggered out of his cabin and shouted a series of incoherent orders at the mate and seven crewmen. As the schooner began to slowly heel to port, two seamen made futile attempts to cut away the masts with an ax.

Vincent Nolte, prominent merchant and adventurer,
shipwrecked off Key Largo in 1808 (drawing from *The
Memoirs of Vincent Nolte,* New York: G. Howard Watt, 1934)

Loud cracking noises spread fear that the vessel was breaking up, and
all hands rushed to launch the longboat. No sooner was the boat in the
water than breaking waves began to fill her. Four seamen climbed down and
were bailing furiously when a huge wave snapped all the lines that held her
alongside. With the four seamen clinging to the gunwales, the boat disappeared into the night. Moments later a cry was heard, "We are aground! We
shall perish!"—then nothing but the roar of the sea.

The jolly boat, a small boat hanging from davits at the stern, was the
only means of escape left. Two seamen lowered it to the water only to see
it dashed to pieces against the hull. As a last resort, the crew assembled sev-

The foremast broke off and fell over the side, carrying the raft with it in a tangle of rigging
(from an illustration in *Blue Jackets of '61* by Willis J. Abbot, New York: Dodd, Meade & Co., 1886)

eral spars and oars and began to lash them together to make a raft. The job was only half finished when the foremast broke off and fell over the side, carrying the raft with it in the tangle of rigging.

As water filled the hull, the schooner slowly rolled over until the deck was more than half submerged and nearly vertical. The only structure available for support was a railing around the starboard side of the quarterdeck. Nolte, his companion, and his manservant, together with the five remaining crew members, lashed themselves to the rail and awaited their fate.

Soaked by the waves and chilled by the wind, the men gradually lost hope. About 4:00 in the morning, they were startled to hear voices. One by one, three figures slowly pulled themselves aboard over the wreckage of the foremast. They were the seamen from the lost longboat. The fourth man, they related, could not swim and had gone down with the boat. They had saved themselves by clinging to the rocks to rest and then wading and swimming until they found the schooner. With their spirits revived by the near-miraculous return of three of their shipmates, the eleven men at the rail waited for the dawn which might bring some means of survival to view. At 7:00 A.M., there was light enough to see low-lying land several miles to the west. They thought it was the Florida mainland, but in fact it was Key Largo.

The seas had subsided sufficiently to allow the men to move about the wreckage, and they set to work to build another raft. In one and a half hours, they had lashed together a makeshift craft of spars, oars, and a chicken coop and had crawled aboard. When all eleven men were on it, the raft sank about two feet in the water and threatened to capsize with the smallest shift in the men's positions. Fortunately, the wind was blowing toward land, and with a sailor holding up a blanket as a sail, the raft drifted slowly away from the wreck.

At about 5:00 in the evening, they saw three small sloops heading toward them. One of the seamen attached his red neckcloth to an oar and waved it overhead, but the sloops, having sighted the wreck, changed course to investigate it. As the light began to fade, the raft drifted near a small island which the survivors later learned was Tavernier Key. They could see three vessels—one of them a large sloop—anchored nearby, but there was no sign of life aboard any of the vessels or onshore.

The sailors tried to paddle toward the vessels, but the raft continued to drift by the island. Just as their hopes were sinking to a new low, they realized the current was carrying them into the lee of a bend in the main

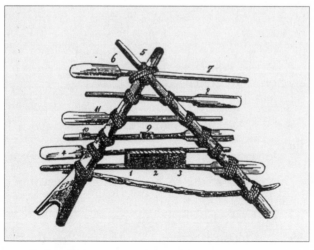

Raft made by survivors of the wreck of the schooner
Merchant. Numbers show the positions occupied by
the eleven crewmen and passengers
(drawing from *The Memoirs of Vincent Nolte,* New York: G. Howard Watt, 1934)

shoreline. At about 10:00 P.M., they discovered that the water was only four feet deep, and two seamen slipped overboard to tow the raft to shore. An hour later, the completely exhausted men staggered onto the beach. Through the long second night of their ordeal, they huddled together to try to restore some warmth to their bodies.

In the morning, the survivors saw the three small sloops anchored near the island they had drifted by the previous evening. They began walking along the shore to get opposite the vessels, a distance of nearly three miles along the beach. No sooner had they started off than they saw the little sloops get underway and sail off. But, an hour later, two of the craft returned and anchored near the large sloop the castaways had seen the night before. By this time, the men had been without anything to eat or drink for thirty-four hours. In their weakened condition, they were forced to stop and rest every five minutes. It was nearly 2:00 in the afternoon before they finally came abreast of the anchored sloops. The survivors could plainly see figures moving about the decks of the vessels, which were about a mile offshore. They shouted and waved a shirt at the top of a long pole, but, incredibly, the crews of the sloops paid no attention to them.

In desperation, Nolte and his companion offered the strongest sailor fifty dollars and a new outfit of clothes if he would attempt to swim out to the sloops. The sailor waded out as far as he could and then began swimming. An hour passed, the sailor's head disappeared from view, and his watching shipmates gave him up for lost. Then, to their great joy, they saw him climb aboard the large sloop and shout over to the men on the smaller craft. In a few minutes, a man from one of the small sloops rowed a skiff over to the large sloop, helped the exhausted sailor into the skiff, and then rowed to the shore.

As small as it was, the skiff was able to hold all the *Merchant's* survivors and carry them out to one of the anchored sloops. When they were safely aboard, the captain of the sloop told them that he and his crew were from the Bahamas. He explained that they had seen the castaways on the beach but were afraid to go to their rescue because they thought the castaways were Spaniards. Not long before, he said, the crew of a Spanish fishing vessel wrecked in the Keys had overpowered their Bahamian rescuers, seized their vessel, and taken it to Cuba. With only four men in each of their crews, the Bahamians were afraid they might meet the same fate if they went to the aid of the men onshore. But when they heard the sailor call to them in English, they felt it was safe to proceed to the rescue.

Unfavorable winds delayed a return to the Bahamas for several days. In the interim, the wreckers salvaged part of the *Merchant*'s cargo and caught some turtles. They also found the wreck of the longboat with the body of the drowned sailor still lashed to his seat. Eleven days after the wreck, Nolte and the rest of the survivors reached Nassau safely.

As the 1800s progressed, the chances of wrecked crews being stranded on their vessels or onshore for more than a day or two became more and more unlikely. When American wreckers took over from the Bahamians, they began regular patrols along the reef, which contributed greatly to saving lives as well as to enriching wrecking vessel owners, captains, and crews.

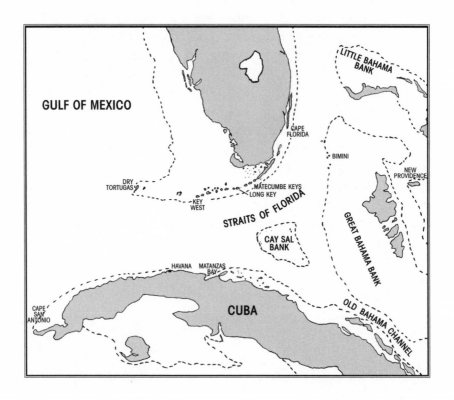

Chapter 3

PRIVATEERS

*P*rivateers were privately owned, armed vessels commissioned by their governments to prey on enemy shipping in wartime. The terms "privateer" and "pirate" are often confused. The misunderstanding is not without basis because some privateers (the same term also applied to the seamen on such vessels) engaged in acts bordering on piracy, and some, after peace was declared, actually became full-time pirates. But most privateers were manned by patriotic citizens who were also highly motivated by the huge profits that might be made.

The government commissioned a privateer by issuing a letter of marque and reprisal. This document authorized the captain to capture enemy ships, their crews, and their cargoes. Warships were usually avoided. The captain was required to post bond against misconduct. After capturing a ship, which was then termed a prize, the privateer's captain had to bring or send the prize back to a port in his own country. There an admiralty court, also called a prize court, would determine whether or not the capture was legal. If illegal, the court would order the vessel to be returned to its owners; if legal, the vessel would be condemned and sold. After deduction of a percentage for the government, the proceeds were divided among the privateer's owners, officers, and crew according to a predetermined formula.

The crew's only pay was their shares of the proceeds from captured prizes. A rich prize could make them wealthy men, but they also faced the possibility of being killed, wounded, or captured and sent to prison.

Privateer vessels might be anything from an open boat to a large, full-rigged ship, but usually they were sizable vessels, heavily manned and armed. Some privateers were specifically designed and built for privateering while others were converted merchantmen. Speed was an all-important factor in their design or selection. They had to be fast enough to catch any merchantman but, more importantly, fast enough to outrun any enemy warship that might chase them. They carried large crews both to man the guns and to provide enough men to man the prizes and bring them back to port.

Many privateer actions took place in the Straits of Florida because of the constricted nature of the passage and the large volume of shipping traffic passing through it. The Spanish treasure flotas (convoyed fleets) passing by the Keys on their return voyages to Spain were an irresistible attraction to English, French, and Dutch privateers. While privateers occasionally picked off stragglers from the convoys, in the main the flota system was successful in bringing gold, silver, and jewels of the New World safely back to Spain. But on one notable occasion in 1628, the system failed.

Capture of Spanish Treasure Flota by Dutch Privateer Fleet
Admiral Piet Heyn, commander of the Dutch West India Company's private fleet of thirty-five warships with over four thousand men, could hardly believe his good fortune. His scout ships had captured nine Spanish courier vessels on their way to Vera Cruz from Havana. From their frightened crews, his officers learned that they had been dispatched to warn the New Spain Flota at Vera Cruz that Heyn's fleet was cruising off Cape San Antonio at the western tip of Cuba. Almost as exciting to Heyn was the information that the flota was commanded by Captain General Juan de Benevides y Bázan, one of his most hated enemies.

Many years earlier, Benevides had been captain of a galley in which Heyn was a prisoner, chained to a rowers' bench. That was the third time Heyn had been forced to serve as a galley slave after being captured by the Spanish. After more than eight years of suffering in chains aboard Spanish galleys, a fire of hatred for Spain and the Spanish burned in Heyn's heart. It had driven him to heroic deeds in sea engagements and to rapid advancement as a naval commander in the employ of the Dutch East India and West India Companies. As a result of his leadership and daring in the capture of twenty-three Portuguese ships under the guns of the forts guarding San Salvador, Brazil, in May 1628, he had been appointed commander of a Dutch West India Company fleet. He vowed to capture an entire Spanish treasure flota.

Heyn's fleet arrived off Cape San Antonio on August 7, 1628. He planned to lie in wait for two treasure galleons expected to sail from Honduras. But when he received intelligence of the imminent sailing of the New Spain Flota, commanded by his sworn enemy, Benevides, he changed his plan. Knowing that the flota would be stopping at Havana, he decided to move his fleet to the vicinity of the Dry Tortugas and wait for his scouting ships to discover the approach of the Spanish fleet. His decision to take station near the Dry Tortugas was not without good reason. Two years earlier, Heyn had been cruising off the Tortugas when ships of a Spanish flota passed so close one night that he could hear the crewmen speaking Spanish.

Dutch warships—In the early 1600s, warships of the Dutch West India Company's privateer fleet lay in wait for Spanish treasure flotas in the vicinity of the Dry Tortugas (from a watercolor by Samuel Van Hoogstraten, 1650. From the collections of The Mariners' Museum, Newport News, Virginia)

Unfortunately, his forces were so few in number that an attack would have been hopeless.

No sooner had the Dutch fleet arrived off the Dry Tortugas than the wind died. The ships drifted helplessly to the southeast. On August 22, they drifted past Havana. Three days later, they were off Matanzas Bay. From a captured Spanish vessel they learned that the New Spain Flota was expected any day.

Taking advantage of every wisp of breeze and every brief squall, the Dutch managed to hold their position off Matanzas. Heyn dispatched his smaller ships, which could be rowed, to make their way towards Havana, forty-five miles to the west, to search for the enemy. Finally, on September 7, a light breeze arose, and the Dutch fleet began to make some headway to the west. During the night, one of the Dutch ships suddenly discovered it was in the middle of the Spanish flota. At first light, the Dutchman, flying Spanish colors, maneuvered to get clear of the flota. As she was leaving, she fired parting broadsides at Benevides' flagship and crowded on sail to carry the news to Heyn.

At daylight, Spanish lookouts sighted the Dutch fleet approaching. Benevides, already shaken up by the gunfire and furious because the pilots had allowed his fleet to drift past Havana, completely lost control of himself. Instead of issuing orders to prepare for battle, he went below to his cabin and began drinking.

By 3:00 in the afternoon, the Dutch fleet was within three miles of the Spanish flota. Benevides finally managed to pull himself together and called a council of his staff officers and captains. Thoroughly intimidated by the size of the Dutch fleet and their well-known fighting ability, the Spanish officers recommended that they sail into Matanzas Bay and transport the treasure ashore. They hoped that after they entered the bay, an offshore evening breeze would prevent the Dutch ships from following them.

No sooner had the Spanish gotten inside the bay than the flagship went aground, followed in short order by the galleon carrying Admiral Loez, second-in-command, followed by two other large galleons. All four galleons were hard aground with their bows pointed towards shore. As a result, only their stern guns could bear on the entrance to the bay.

The Dutch ships reached the entrance just as the onshore breeze failed.

They anchored and began firing at the Spanish ships. When it became apparent that the four galleons were aground, Heyn ordered the boats lowered and, leading the way, rowed towards them intending to take them by boarding. When Benevides saw the Dutch boats being lowered, he lost whatever small bit of courage he had remaining and gave the order to the flota's crew to abandon their ships and make for shore. More concerned to save his own skin than the king's treasure, he was the first one over the side.

Heyn directed his boats to head for the largest galleon, assuming it was the flagship. Actually, it was the flagship of the second-in-command, Admiral Don Juan de Leoz. Leoz had about the same amount of courage as his commander. When he saw the Dutch boats approaching his ship, he quickly took off his uniform and put on seaman's clothes to hide his identity.

At 9:00 P.M., the Dutch boats were in position to board. They fired a volley and called out in Spanish that they would grant quarter. The demoralized and leaderless Spanish crew immediately surrendered. As soon as Heyn discovered that the galleon he had boarded was not Benevides' ship, he directed the boat crews to row him rapidly to the next galleon, which, in fact, was the flagship. Once again, those left onboard gave up without firing a shot. When Heyn discovered that Benevides had already left the ship, he almost wept with frustration and rage.

All the treasure galleons and merchant ships in the bay—seventeen in all—surrendered without putting up a fight. Nine other merchant ships had been captured the previous day after they became separated from the main flota and fled towards Havana. Of the entire flota, only one small merchant ship escaped.

The loss of the New Spain Flota was a terrible calamity for Spain. In June, the Spanish government was forced to declare bankruptcy. For the Dutch, the victory paved the way towards winning complete independence from Spain.

During the return voyage home, the Dutch fleet suffered a number of calamities. They ran into bad weather and lost a captured galleon, but not before they transferred the treasure it was carrying to another ship. The Dutch crews were stricken with scurvy and other diseases and so were ill-prepared to fight off some Dunkirk privateers that attacked them in the

Capture of Spanish treasure flota in Matanzas Bay, Cuba, by the Dutch West India Company's privateer fleet under Admiral Piet Heyn in September 1628. Inset upper left: Admiral Piet Heyn. Inset upper right: Admiral Hendrik Loncq, second-in command. (courtesy of Rijksmuseum, Amsterdam)

English Channel. Nevertheless, they brought the treasure safely to a Dutch port. Heyn received a hero's welcome and was appointed commander of the Dutch Navy. But just five months after his triumphal return, he was killed in action fighting a group of Flemish privateers. All of the Dutch nation went into mourning for thirty days. Even today, Admiral Piet Heyn is revered as one of the Netherlands' greatest heroes.

Benevides returned to Spain a prisoner and was condemned to death, as was his second-in-command, Leoz. Only the fact that Benevides' sister was the king's mistress saved the two admirals from immediate execution. Six years later, when his sister died, Benevides was publicly beheaded and Leoz was permanently banished to an outpost in North Africa.

European Settlements and Wars Give Rise to Privateering in the Caribbean

As the English, French, and Dutch established settlements in the Caribbean from the 1620s to 1650s, their ships returning to Europe through the Straits of Florida became prey to Spanish privateers. In the late 1600s,

American colonial ships trading in the West Indies added to the parade of rich prizes that could be found in the Straits. During the wars of the French Revolution, Bahamian privateers frequented the Keys in search of Spanish ships. In 1799, in a period of a little more than a week, an American survey ship in the Keys met two Bahamian privateers and two captured Spanish prizes manned by Bahamian crews.

Despite Spanish prohibitions against it, English privateers began making voyages to trade with or raid Spanish colonies in America in the 1560s. Often they returned home by way of the Straits of Florida. John Hawkins, returning from his second voyage in 1565, stopped in the Dry Tortugas to capture turtles and somewhere in the Keys to find water. His boat crews found water but were very nearly lost when the ships became caught in the Florida Current and drifted away.

Sir Francis Drake, who like the other English privateers was called a pirate by the Spanish, sailed into the Straits in 1586 in search of a Spanish treasure fleet. Failing to intercept the galleons and finding Havana too well

Sir Francis Drake and Sir John Hawkins,
English privateers who challenged Spain's monopoly in the Caribbean (*Harper's New Monthly Magazine,* Vol. CXI, July 1905. From the collections of The Mariners' Museum, Newport News, Virginia)

defended, he sailed along the Keys, continued up the coast of Florida, and sacked St. Augustine. Another early English privateer, Christopher Newport, stopped in the Keys in 1592 to obtain water. During his return from a successful cruise in the West Indies, he sacked four Spanish towns and captured nineteen Spanish ships. While he was taking on water at one of the Keys, a Spanish ship had the misfortune to sail in, seeking shelter from heavy weather. Newport captured the ship and relieved her of her cargo of hogs and tobacco. Two years earlier, a French privateer wrecked in the Keys suffered an even worse fate. A Spanish ship discovered the castaway crew and took them to Havana, where they were hanged.

Like the Spanish, the English formed large convoys to guard their merchant ships returning home through the Straits during wartime. In 1697, an English convoy passing through the Straits was comprised of 116 merchant ships escorted by 6 warships.

During the 1600s and 1700s, European wars spilled over into the Caribbean and sparked a number of privateer actions in the waters off the Keys. King William's War (England, Holland, and Spain against France

European wars in the 1600s and 1700s spilled over into the Caribbean and sparked many privateer actions in the Straits of Florida (*Harper's New Monthly Magazine,* Vol. V, June 1852. From the collections of The Mariners' Museum, Newport News, Virginia)

from 1689 to 1697) marked the first time American colonial privateers participated extensively in commerce raiding. They were active again in the War of Spanish Succession, with England, Austria, and Holland fighting Spain and France from 1702 to 1713. Following the peace treaty, large numbers of privateers turned to piracy and used New Providence in the Bahamas as their base of operations.

During the War of Jenkins' Ear (1739–1743) between England and Spain, American colonists fitted out hundreds of privateers to raid commerce in the Caribbean and elsewhere. Two notable engagements by colonial privateers during that war took place in the Straits of Florida in 1742. Their stories follow.

Colonial Privateers Intercept Spanish Transports in the Keys
"Sail ho!" cried the lookout at *Young Eagle*'s masthead.

The captain sprang to the mainmast rigging and climbed the ratlines to the crosstrees. For a few minutes he studied the horizon through his telescope, then called down to the deck, "Signal *Bonetta* we have eight enemy

The captain sprang to the mainmast rigging and climbed the ratlines to the crosstrees
(drawing by Wayne Giordano)

sail in sight to the northwest, and call all hands on deck to clear for action."

Thus began a fortunate day for two colonial privateers northward bound off the upper Keys on August 19, 1742. The *Young Eagle* was a one-hundred-ton, twelve-gun bilander (two-masted with mainmast lateen-rigged and foremast square-rigged) out of Boston, Massachusetts. She was commanded by John Rouse, a daring and highly successful privateer captain who had begun his privateering career three years earlier as one of *Young Eagle*'s lieutenants. Hot-tempered, he had been imprisoned briefly for insubordination but, having proved his worth in action, succeeded to command when *Young Eagle*'s first captain died.

In company with *Young Eagle* was the sloop *Bonetta,* commanded by Robert Flowers, out of St. Kitts, a British colony in the leeward islands. The two privateers were returning to New England after a cruise in the Caribbean during which they had taken two prizes. A third member of the little privateer fleet, the sloop *Mary,* had become separated from the group several days earlier.

Young Eagle and *Bonetta* set a course to intercept the enemy vessels which were part of a large Spanish fleet returning from an unsuccessful attack on the English settlement at St. Simon, Georgia. Most of the Spanish ships were lightly armed merchantmen transporting soldiers and arms of the expedition back to Havana. The chase continued for eight hours. Near nightfall, four of the Spanish ships crossed the reef and entered a shallow bay at the eastern end of *Cayo de Vivoras* (Long Key). Rouse and Flowers anchored their ships at the entrance to be ready to attack in the morning. The other four Spanish vessels, with lighter drafts, had sailed into shallow waters among the Keys and were out of reach.

At first light, the two privateers made sail and approached the Spanish vessels in the bay as close as their deeper drafts allowed. They saw that two of them, a sloop and a schooner, were aground. The other two schooners, smaller in size, had anchored in shallow water further away. *Young Eagle* fired several shots at the small schooners, but, after one of them moved closer inshore and reanchored, both were out of range. The privateers then directed their fire against the grounded sloop and schooner. Some of the Spanish crewmen jumped overboard and swam ashore while others escaped in a boat. After returning a few shots, both Spanish vessels struck their colors. Rouse and Flowers sent their lieutenants in boats to secure the prizes. Upon boarding, they found that the sloop, armed with six carriage guns, had been abandoned by her captain. An infantry lieutenant was in charge of the remaining soldiers and seamen. The schooner, with only two swivel guns for defense, was still manned by her captain, crewmen, and about thirty soldiers.

Flowers went aboard the prizes soon thereafter. As he was inspecting them, he sighted another sloop sailing along the reef about six miles distant. Forcing one of the Spanish officers to come with him, Flowers immediately returned to the *Bonetta*, weighed anchor, and took up chase. Using dire threats, he coerced his prisoner into revealing the Spanish recognition signals and hoisted the appropriate flags. The enemy sloop answered the signal and changed course to head toward the *Bonetta*. But as she drew closer, her captain recognized *Bonetta* as an English-built vessel and altered course to escape.

After a two-hour chase, the *Bonetta* came within gun range and fired two broadsides, and the Spanish sloop surrendered. She was the *Rosa,* carrying about forty soldiers in addition to her regular crew. She had been armed with six carriage guns, but the captain had ordered them heaved overboard during his attempt to escape. Soon afterwards, the *Young Eagle,* with the two Spanish prizes in company, arrived on the scene. All five vessels then stood into the shelter of the Keys and anchored for the night.

In the morning, Rouse and Flowers conferred and agreed that they did not have enough provisions and water to take all their prisoners back to New England. They decided to put all the Spaniards—except the officers they would need to testify at the prize court proceedings—aboard the *Rosa*, the least valuable of the three Spanish vessels. They would then release the *Rosa* to return to Havana. As they were transferring the prisoners to the *Rosa* and taking off her arms and ammunition, a lookout sighted five more sloops to the east. Both colonial captains hoisted Spanish colors, hoping to lure the vessels closer. When the foremost sloops were about three miles distant, Rouse got the *Young Eagle* under way and took up chase.

Driving before a strong wind, Rouse's ship gradually closed on the Spaniards. Two of the five sloops managed to escape into shallow water where the *Young Eagle* could not follow. The other three piled up on the reef off the Matecumbe Keys. Owing to the force of the wind and the height of the seas, Rouse decided it was too dangerous to send boats in to capture them. He returned to anchor by *Bonetta* and the three Spanish prizes.

The next morning, the two privateer captains released the *Rosa* to return to Havana with the freed Spanish soldiers and seamen. As the colonial captains began their voyage back to New England, they passed the Matecumbe Keys. They could see that the three Spanish sloops were still hard aground on the reef and broadside to the breaking seas. A fourth Spanish vessel had anchored in shallow water nearby. The seas were still too high to risk sending in boats, and the two captains reluctantly departed, believing the vessels on the reef would soon break up.

Young Eagle, Bonetta, and their prizes safely reached Newport, Rhode Island, having managed to avoid Spanish privateers operating along the eastern seaboard. At the admiralty court proceedings, the captured Spanish officers testified that their vessels were, in fact, Spanish ships in the service of the King of Spain. The court ruled that the captures were legal, and the prizes were condemned and sold.

One year later, in 1743, the French entered the war on Spain's side. Rouse, still in command of *Young Eagle,* led three other privateers in a battle against five well-armed French ships. After a six-hour fight, the French surrendered, yielding—among other cargo—ninety cannon.

Rouse also commanded another highly successful privateer, the *Speedwell,* and was captain of the twenty-four-gun Massachusetts coast defense ship *Shirley* during the attack on the French fortress of Louisbourg in Nova Scotia in 1745. He was cited for distinguished service in capturing eight French ships and was awarded a captain's commission in the Royal Navy. Nothing further is known of Robert Flowers' career.

One-Armed Colonial Captain Battles Spanish Privateer to a Draw

If ever misfortune dogged the steps of a man, that man's name was James Wimble. Mariner, trader, land developer, distiller, chart maker, and privateer captain, Captain Wimble, despite one reversal of fortune after another, never gave up.

Born in England in 1697, he began to follow the sea at an early age.

When he was twenty-one he built his own vessel with the help of friends and sailed across the Atlantic to seek his fortune in the West Indies. Not long after arriving, he lost his ship—the first of four vessels he was to lose in his lifetime—probably on an uncharted shoal.

Undaunted, Wimble found employment as master of a small merchant sloop. For the next fifteen years, he prospered by making trading voyages between the West Indies and the American colonies in command of several different vessels. On one of these voyages in 1728, his ship was seized by the Spanish and, as far as is known, was never recovered. Between voyages, he found time to marry a Boston girl, buy a distillery, sire five children, and purchase land in the Bahamas and North Carolina.

The captain's second major setback came in 1732. Two years earlier he had purchased a newly launched, 128-ton brigantine which he named *Rebecca* after his wife. He manned her with a crew of fourteen and fitted her out with ten guns for protection against the Spanish *guarda-costas* and privateers who were molesting British shipping in the Caribbean. On a voyage from North Carolina to Boston in December of 1731, Wimble encountered a storm which severely damaged his ship. With a serious leak threatening to sink the *Rebecca,* Wimble turned and ran before the gale, eventually arriving in Jamaica. After making repairs, he headed north again through the Straits of Florida. Another storm and a grounding near Bimini forced him to put in to New Providence in the Bahamas for repairs.

When Wimble was ready to resume his voyage, the governor refused to give him permission to depart. Two weeks later, the governor ordered the *Rebecca* into government service to protect the workers at the salt ponds on Rum Cay against Spanish raids. While Wimble was in this service, the collector of customs at New Providence fined him two hundred pounds on trumped-up charges of violating customs regulations. Wimble had to sell his slaves and cargo to pay the fine. The final blow to his fortunes came in August of 1732, when a hurricane hurled his ship ashore on Rum Cay and broke her to pieces. Throughout the remainder of his short life, Wimble made numerous attempts to obtain compensation for the loss of his ship while in enforced government service. He even made a voyage to London to plead his case. But all his efforts were to no avail. Bureaucratic evasions defeated him in every instance.

One year after the loss of the *Rebecca,* despite being heavily in debt, Wimble entered into a partnership with three other men to buy land for a settlement near the mouth of the Cape Fear River in North Carolina. About the same time, he completed and published a chart of the North Carolina coast, which was acclaimed as the best of its time.

With sales of lots going well in the town that was to become Wilmington, Wimble returned to making trading voyages to the Caribbean. About this time, relations between England and Spain had reached a near breaking point over Spanish harassment of British shipping in the West Indies. In a letter written in 1735, Wimble said that the Spaniards had "taken" him seven times. Whether this meant that they had stopped and boarded him, seized his cargo, or seized his ship is not clear, but he was so upset that he threatened to leave the sea. These incidents further inflamed Wimble's hatred of the Spanish and his determination to have revenge.

Four years later, in 1739, England declared war against Spain. With his petition for redress in the case of the *Rebecca* denied for the third time and his wife dead, Wimble, still heavily in debt, decided to try to recoup his losses by going privateering. In 1741, he took command of an eighteen-gun privateer which he named *Revenge*. But less than a year later, with his usual bad luck, he ran onto a reef at Antlings Key in the Bahamas and lost his third ship.

Discouraged but undeterred from his mission, he returned to New Providence where he purchased a sloop, a former Spanish privateer which had been captured by a British frigate. The sloop came armed with ten carriage guns and ten swivel guns. Wimble recruited a crew of forty seamen and, ignoring superstition, again chose *Revenge* for her name. Shortly after putting to sea, Wimble met up with a Rhode Island privateer, the *St. Andrew,* commanded by Captain Davidson. Wimble and Davidson entered into an agreement to cruise together and share whatever prizes they took. Their first captures were four small Spanish schooners that they manned with prize crews and sent to New Providence.

Two days later, they met a more formidable adversary, a thirty-gun Spanish ship with a large crew determined to put up a fight. While waiting for the *St. Andrew* to join him, Wimble maneuvered astern of the Spanish ship and peppered her with shots from his bow chaser. The Spaniard returned fire with a stern gun. The exchange of fire continued for two hours, at which point a chain shot (two cannon balls linked by a short piece of chain) from the Spanish ship severed Wimble's left arm five inches below the shoulder.

Fearing his crew would lose heart and give up the fight, Wimble somehow managed to conceal the loss of his arm for a short while. But after losing a great deal of blood, he fainted and was carried below deck. His lieutenant lowered a boat and carried the news of Wimble's wound to Captain Davidson. The two men agreed it would be best to abandon the attempt to take the Spaniard and to get Wimble back to New Providence for medical aid.

Driven by a burning desire to make the Spanish pay for his injuries and by a pressing need to recoup his finances, Wimble recuperated rapidly. In two months time, he was back at sea. He soon captured a Spanish vessel, put five of his men aboard to sail her, and took ten Spanish crewmen onboard as prisoners. This left him with only eighteen men and boys to handle *Revenge*. On July 14, 1742, while cruising in the northern end of the Straits of Florida, the lookout sighted a sail. On closing with her, Wimble saw she was a Spanish privateer with ten or twelve carriage guns, an equal number of swivel guns, and a crew of about seventy men. Despite being outnumbered four to one, Wimble did not hesitate to engage.

The wind was nearly calm, so there was no possibility of either ship maneuvering to gain a favorable position. For an hour and a half, the two exchanged cannon and musket fire at point-blank range, variously reported as twenty feet to thirty yards. The Spaniards attempted to board the *Revenge* several times but were beaten back. Had they been able to get aboard, they certainly would have taken her. That they did not was almost entirely due to Captain Wimble's courage and indomitable fighting spirit. Taking a crowbar in his one hand, he leveled (pointed) each of the guns as they were loaded. His well-aimed shots killed the Spanish captain and thirty of his crewmen. Another shot parted the Spaniard's topsail sheets. The topsail swung around, became backwinded, and caused the Spanish ship to lose steerageway. One more shot parted the topping lift for the mainsail boom. The boom and sail fell on deck, preventing the use of the after guns until the wreckage could be cleared away. While the Spaniards were busy with

Wimble decided to engage the Spanish privateer despite being
outnumbered four to one (redrawn by Wayne Giordano from an illustration in
A History of American Privateers by Edgar S. Stanton, New York: D. Appleton and Co., 1899)

their downed mainsail and boom, Wimble ordered his men to get out the
sweeps (long oars). Using these, they turned the *Revenge* around and gave
the Spanish ship a fresh broadside.

But all was not well on the *Revenge*. In the midst of the battle, the
Spanish prisoners below deck attempted to come on deck and take the ship
but failed. As the fighting progressed, the gun tackles were shot away one
by one. One hundred and twenty shots (counted after the battle) from the
Spanish ship had struck the *Revenge's* sails, mast, and hull, inflicting serious
damage. Unbelievably, despite the hail of cannon and musket balls, not a
single crewman on the *Revenge* had been killed or wounded. After two hours

of fierce fighting, the exhausted English and Spanish crews ceased firing at each other, and, as if by mutual consent, the ships slowly drew apart and went their separate ways.

While Wimble was engaging the Spanish privateer, his prize crew had sailed the captured Spanish vessel well clear of the action. After the battle, Wimble rejoined his prize, manned her with thirteen of his crew, and armed her with a carriage gun and four swivels. The two privateers then sailed to Port-au-Prince, where they sank seven Spanish vessels and captured one loaded with sugar. Wimble returned to New Providence, where his two prizes were condemned and sold. From the proceeds, he distributed 150 pieces of eight to each of his crewmen.

Because of the weakened condition of *Revenge's* spars and rigging, Wimble returned to Charleston for a complete refit, narrowly escaping two Spanish privateers on the way. He put to sea again sometime in early 1743. In April, he met another Rhode Island privateer, also named *Revenge,* off the north coast of Cuba. The two *Revenge*s joined forces and, two weeks later, captured a 240-ton frigate off Havana after a stiff fight. The frigate proved to be a former English ship loaded with a valuable cargo of sugar, mahogany, cotton, ivory, ginger, and ammunition. The two privateers escorted their prize safely back to Newport.

Once again, Wimble put to sea to exact his due from the Spaniards. In November of 1743, he arrived in New Providence. Less than a month later, fate dealt its final blow. The *Revenge* ran aground on some rocks off the coast of Hispaniola and was lost. Whether Wimble died as a direct result of being shipwrecked or of despair soon thereafter is not known. In March 1744, some property of James Wimble, "mariner deceased," was sold at auction in New Hanover County, North Carolina. Ironically, the only lasting memorial to this four-time shipwrecked captain and his indomitable fighting spirit is a treacherous submerged sandbar north of Cape Hatteras named Wimble Shoals.

American Privateers in the American Revolution

At the beginning of the War of Independence, the colonists had no navy. It was only natural that they would turn to privateering as a means to prosecute the war at sea. One authority puts the number of American privateers commissioned at more than two thousand. A researcher who surveyed newspapers of six states found that 2,106 prizes were sent to American ports. The British Navy was forced to divert a large number of its warships from home defense tasks to convoy duty and anti-privateer patrols. While American privateer captures did not win the war at sea, they contributed significantly to building sentiment against the war among the British merchant class.

Throughout the war, American privateers passed through or patrolled the Straits of Florida. The first private ships of war to be fitted out by the colonies, the Pennsylvania sloops *Congress* and *Chance,* captured three British ships in the Straits in May 1776. In July 1777, the American privateers *Vixen* and *Washington* cut a merchant ship out of a British convoy consisting of one hundred merchantmen escorted by four warships and brought her into Havana. In 1778, two American privateers chased the British ship *Mary* onto the reef off Cape Florida, where she was lost. Alexander Murray, in command of the Virginia privateer brig *Prosperity,* captured a British packet ship in the Straits in early 1782 and then took part in the capture of Nassau. By no means were all the American privateer cruises successful. The vastly superior British Navy captured hundreds of American privateers, and thousands of captured American seamen experienced the horrors of life onboard British prison ships, where many of them died.

After a prize was taken, the problem of getting it safely back to an American port remained. Not only was there the danger that the prize would be recaptured by an enemy warship or privateer, there was also the possibility that the prisoners onboard might retake their ship, as happened in the case of the *Polly and Nancy.*

Peter Norris Versus the Polly and Nancy

One of the most unusual series of events in the history of American privateering actions during the Revolutionary War took place in the waters off the Dry Tortugas in January 1778. The story of these events is contained in the testimony of the prize court case, "Peter Norris and Others vs. Schooner *Polly and Nancy,*" which was heard in admiralty court at Charles

Town, South Carolina, in February and March 1778. Unfortunately, the witnesses left gaps in their narratives and failed to explain the reasons for certain puzzling actions they took. As a result, some parts of the story can only be guessed at.

The story begins in November 1777 when the forty-ton American privateer sloop *Rutledge* got under way from Charles Town on a cruise. She was manned by seventy-seven officers and men under the command of John Porter. Among the crewmen was Peter Norris, who signed on as prize master. A prize master was a mariner qualified to serve as master and navigator of captured vessels for the purpose of bringing them back to an American port.

Two weeks after sailing, the *Rutledge* captured a British sloop named *Pallas*. She must have been a well-built vessel and a fast sailer, because Porter decided to keep her as a tender or auxiliary privateer rather than send her in as a prize. He transferred several cannon and a quantity of arms onboard, manned her with some of *Rutledge's* men, including Peter Norris, and placed his second lieutenant, Matthew Smith, in command. Whether the *Pallas'* small crew remained aboard as prisoners or were transferred to the *Rutledge* is not stated.

After cruising together for several weeks off the northern coast of Cuba without taking any prizes, the *Rutledge* sighted a large group of ships and gave chase. It was two weeks before she returned empty-handed. In the meantime, the *Pallas* had captured a small schooner. Captain Porter ordered Peter Norris to take command of the prize. A gale separated the three ships a few days later. *Pallas* and the prize schooner soon found each other, but the *Rutledge* never reappeared.

About the same time these events were taking place in early January, an unarmed merchant schooner, the *Polly and Nancy* of Jamaica, left Mobile (then under British control) and headed south to return to Kingston. The thirty-ton vessel was loaded with twenty thousand staves and headings (used to make barrels) and manned by a crew of five. Her captain, John Davis, was also half-owner. William Williamson, the other half-owner, was onboard as a passenger.

On January 17, a lookout on the *Pallas* sighted a sail, and Smith gave chase. The *Pallas* quickly overtook a deeply laden schooner which proved to be the *Polly and Nancy*. Lacking any means of resistance, Captain Davis had no choice but to surrender. Davis, his five crewmen, and passenger Williamson were brought aboard the *Pallas* and made prisoners. Smith then ordered Norris and four seamen to take over the *Polly and Nancy* as prize crew and proceed to Charles Town. The three vessels were still close together when night fell. During the night, Norris heard gunfire from the direction of the *Pallas*. Suspecting that the prisoners might have retaken her and having no arms to come to Smith's aid, he crowded on sail to escape.

Norris' suspicions were correct. Some members of the *Pallas'* crew, apparently Tories at heart, had mutinied and released the prisoners and were now in command of the ship under the leadership of Captain Davis. At first light, Davis hauled the *Pallas* alongside the small schooner and recap-

Boarding party from American privateer *Pallas* captures British merchant schooner *Polly and Nancy* (drawing by Wayne Giordano)

tured her. One day later he sighted the *Polly and Nancy*, quickly overtook her, and recaptured her also. Davis ordered Norris to come aboard the *Pallas*, telling him if he opened his mouth to speak he would lose his head. Norris replied that he understood he was a prisoner and would behave as such.

A little while later, Davis had Norris brought to his cabin and began a conversation with him. He offered Norris a drink, and the two men continued talking and drinking for some time. Finally Davis asked Norris if he would be interested in taking the *Polly and Nancy* to Jamaica as master and navigator, presumably for a consideration. Norris said he would be willing to do it. To be sure Norris did not change his mind, Davis had his partner, William Williamson, and one of his crewmen, James Cavannah, go along with Norris and his four-man crew to keep an eye on them. The three vessels then set sail for Jamaica together.

The next day, however, Davis came alongside the *Polly and Nancy* and told Norris to change course and head for Mobile. Davis may have decided that the long voyage back to Jamaica was too risky and that he might lose not only the *Polly and Nancy* again, but his two prizes as well. For the next four days, the three vessels continued sailing together. On several occasions, Davis brought *Pallas* alongside the *Polly and Nancy* and reminded Norris that if he made any attempt to part company, Davis would blow his brains out the next time he caught up with him.

On the fifth day after changing course for Mobile, Norris saw the opportunity he had been waiting for. Although he does not describe the circumstances in his testimony, the vessels might have drifted further apart than usual when night fell, or a gale might have separated them. In any event, Norris and his four crewmen overpowered Williamson and Cavannah when their guard was down and, setting every available sail, headed eastward through the Straits of Florida.

Three weeks later, the *Polly and Nancy* dropped anchor at George Town, South Carolina. Norris promptly made his way to Charles Town and engaged a lawyer to present his claim to the *Polly and Nancy* as prize to himself and his four crewmen. Norris reasoned that since he had captured the vessel while she was in the possession of one of her original British owners, he was entitled to make her his prize.

Unfortunately for Norris, the *Rutledge* and Captain Porter had also returned to Charles Town. Captain Porter filed a countersuit claiming the *Polly and Nancy* as rightful prize of the owners, officers, and crew of the *Rutledge*. He contended that Norris, like all the crewmembers of the privateer, had signed articles at the beginning of the cruise in which he agreed that all prizes taken on the cruise would be divided among the owners, officers, and crews in the proportions set forth in the articles.

The case was submitted to a jury, which ruled in favor of the owners, officers, and men of the *Rutledge*. Instead of sharing the proceeds of the sale of the *Polly and Nancy* and her cargo—a princely sum—with his four crewmen, Norris received only one share of one half of the money divided among seventy-seven crewmen and officers. One wonders if it would have been enough to pay his lawyer's fee.

American Privateers in the War of 1812

Once again, in 1812, America fought a war with a weak navy. Whereas only 22 warships were commissioned during the war, 538 privateer commissions were issued. Privateering was more effective in the War of 1812 than in any other. By 1814, American privateers, operating mainly in the West Indies and the waters around the British Isles, had captured more than sixteen hundred British ships. Marine insurance rates doubled, then tripled. Because of their heavy losses, British shipping interests demanded that their government bring the war to an end.

America, an American privateer of the War of 1812 (watercolor by Antoine Roux. Courtesy of Peabody Essex Museum, Salem, Massachusetts)

As before, privateers did everything in their power to avoid enemy warships. When they failed to escape, they were almost always captured, often without a shot. A rare exception to this rule occurred in the Straits of Florida in 1814, when one of the most bold and daring privateersmen of the war unexpectedly came across a British Navy schooner-of-war.

Duel in the Straits—American Privateer Versus British Man-of-War

Thomas Boyle of Baltimore was one of the most daring and successful privateer captains of the War of 1812. He began his career in command of the privateer *Comet* and on his first cruise took three large British ships which, together with their cargoes, were worth nearly a half million dollars. He made three cruises with the *Comet*—a total of twenty-one months at sea— and captured twenty-seven prizes.

In 1814, he took command of the Baltimore-built topsail schooner, *Chasseur,* one of the fastest and best equipped privateers of the war. A writer for a Baltimore newspaper said, "As you look at her you may easily figure to yourself the idea that she is almost about to rise out of the water and fly into the air." Armed with 16 twelve-pounder long guns, she was 116 feet long and manned by a crew of 150 officers and men.

Boyle was a very strict but fair captain. He ran his ship like a man-of-war. Unlike most other privateers, he drilled the crew at the guns and small arms daily and practiced sail handling under difficult maneuvering conditions. On his first cruise in *Chasseur,* he took eighteen prizes in three months while cruising in the waters around the British Isles. He also had several narrow escapes from British men-of-war. On one occasion, he was surrounded by two frigates and two brigs-of-war yet managed to get away.

Returning to Baltimore in October 1814, Boyle decided to try his luck in the Caribbean again rather than attempt a North Atlantic cruise in wintertime. He substituted carronades (short-barreled guns) for ten of his long twelve-pounders because he expected to be fighting at closer ranges and carronades could be fired more rapidly. He also modified his masts and spars so that he could change his rig from schooner to brig, or brigantine, to deceive the enemy.

Chasseur broke through the British blockade on December 23, 1814, and headed south for Barbados. Unbeknownst to Boyle, a peace treaty was signed in Ghent, Belgium, the next day. Fortunately for him, a provision of the treaty made all captures valid for thirty days after Congress ratified the treaty.

On January 30, 1815, in the vicinity of Martinique, a fast British frigate gave chase to *Chasseur*. Driving before heavy squalls and high seas, conditions which favored the larger ship, the frigate slowly closed the range. Boyle ordered his crew to heave the ten carronades and some of the spare spars overboard. The gun crews hauled two of the long guns aft, cut away part of the taffrail around the stern, and fired at the frigate's rigging. A lucky shot carried away some of her rigging, the wind began to moderate, and *Chasseur* slowly pulled away from her pursuer.

Early in February, Boyle captured a well-armed merchant ship after a short fight. He took aboard eight of the prize's nine-pounder carronades as partial replacement for the ten twelve-pounder carronades he had heaved overboard. Not only was his armament significantly reduced, but the transfer of men to man prizes had shrunk his crew to just over one hundred officers and men.

A few days later, the Baltimore privateer sighted a British convoy of 110 merchantmen escorted by several men-of-war. For the next three weeks, Boyle trailed the convoy and took two stragglers from it. The convoy sailed north through the Yucatan Straits and then headed east for Havana. Sometimes Boyle would lose sight of the convoy for several days but always managed to find it again. On February 27, with the convoy once more in sight near Havana, a lookout reported two sails to windward. After overtaking the first sail, which proved to be a Russian brig, Boyle set off in pursuit of the second.

As the *Chasseur* drew closer to the stranger, Boyle could see she was a large topsail schooner with all sails set, apparently trying to escape. When *Chasseur* continued to close the range, the schooner changed course to sail closer to the wind, expecting that *Chasseur,* then rigged as a brigantine, would not be able to match her course to windward. As the schooner heeled before the fresh breeze, her topmast carried away. *Chasseur* closed rapidly while the schooner's crew was clearing away the wreckage. Observing that there were just a few hands on the schooner's deck and only three gun ports in her side, Boyle assumed she was a merchant vessel. He ordered the guns manned but, not expecting a fight, did not clear for action. He directed one of his forward gun crews to fire a shot and hoisted the American colors. The schooner replied with a stern gun and hoisted the British colors.

Chasseur continued to close the schooner until she was nearly abreast and within pistol shot range. Suddenly, not three but ten gun ports in the schooner's side opened and erupted fire. A full broadside of grape and round shot struck the *Chasseur* with such force that she heeled over. A large number of men who had been concealed behind the schooner's bulwarks rose and began firing with muskets. Among them, Boyle could see officers in the uniform of the Royal Navy. With musket balls thudding into the deck around him and a splinter wound in his arm, he realized that he was dealing with a British man-of war. Instead of sheering off and escaping as his superior speed would have allowed him to do, he chose to stay and fight. As he expressed it in his report to *Chasseur's* owners, "I should not willingly perhaps have sought a contest with a king's vessel knowing it was not our object, but my expectations were at first a valuable vessel and a valuable cargo. When I found myself deceived, the honor of the flag left with me was not to be disgraced by flight."

Boyle's superbly trained crew got off a return broadside almost immediately, and the firing became rapid and heavy on both vessels. Men fell beside their guns—some dead, others with gaping wounds—while spars and rigging crashed down among them. Blood streamed across the decks and even ran from the scuppers.

Boyle steered to close with the British schooner and board her but, because of his faster speed, shot ahead and off to leeward. The British captain quickly put his helm up to wear (turn away from the wind) and to be in a position to rake the American's stern. Boyle detected the enemy's intention as soon as the schooner began to turn and put his helm up also. When the maneuvers were completed, both vessels were again running on parallel courses, with *Chasseur* to windward and close aboard. Once more, the privateer and the man-of-war, now just ten yards apart, exchanged broadsides and musket fire, inflicting heavy damage and killing and wounding more men on both vessels.

Boyle still thought his best chance to end the carnage was to board. He

Capture of HMS *St. Lawrence* by the Baltimore privateer *Chasseur* (lithograph published by A. Weingarthers. From the collections of The Mariners' Museum, Newport News, Virginia)

ordered a boarding party to stand by and steered the *Chasseur* in toward the schooner until the bow scraped alongside. Just as the first man leaped aboard the British schooner, her flag came down. In an unprecedented action lasting only fifteen minutes, an American privateer had defeated a British man-of-war, His Britannic Majesty's Schooner *St. Lawrence*.

Ironically, *St. Lawrence* was a former American privateer which had been captured by the British and refitted as a warship. She was very nearly the same size as *Chasseur*. Her armament of fourteen twelve-pounders and one long nine-pounder could fire double the weight of shot of *Chasseur's* guns. She was manned by a crew of 75, compared to *Chasseur's* 102. All things considered, the two vessels were very nearly equal in fighting power, but the results of the action told a different story. The *St. Lawrence* lost six men killed and seventeen wounded, three of them mortally, and all her officers were among the dead and wounded. As Boyle described it, she was "reduced to a perfect wreck, cut to pieces in the hull, with scarcely a rope left standing." That night, her weakened masts went overboard. The heavy damage suffered by the *St. Lawrence* bore testimony to the accuracy and rapid rate of fire of the Boyle-trained gun crews.

On the *Chasseur*, five men were killed and eight wounded, including Boyle. Although she was damaged, mainly in the rigging and sails, her crew was able to make repairs to allow her to continue on her way. After *Chasseur's* surgeon had taken care of her wounded, Boyle sent him across to the *St. Lawrence* to assist the British surgeon. In view of the serious condition of his wounded men, *St. Lawrence's* captain, Lieutenant Gordon, asked Boyle for permission to proceed into Havana under a flag of truce to put them ashore. He also gave his word that he would not attempt to retake his ship and would turn her over to Boyle's prize master afterwards. Boyle, a true gentleman, gave his permission.

The *Chasseur* headed northeast through the Straits of Florida for home. On March 15, she met an American brig and learned that the peace treaty had been ratified and signed by President Madison on February 17. She sailed into Baltimore harbor to the cheers of a large crowd on March 20. The British sailed the *St. Lawrence* to Bermuda where an admiralty court ruled that, in accordance with the terms of peace, she was to be returned to the United States as a legitimate prize of war.

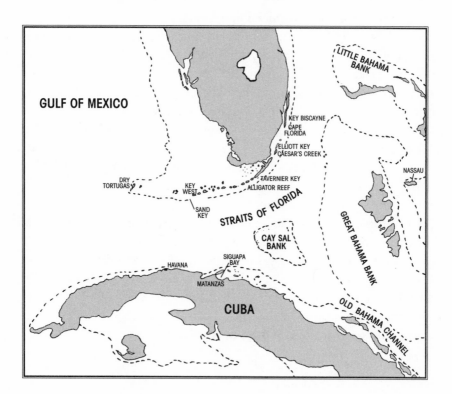

Chapter 4

PIRATES AND PIRATE HUNTERS

Pirate Eras

*F*or more than three hundred years, beginning with the passage of the first Spanish treasure galleons, piracy was one more of the many hazards facing vessels voyaging through the Straits of Florida. Twice during that span of centuries, piracy in the Caribbean, Gulf of Mexico, and along the Atlantic Coast reached epidemic proportions. The first outbreak began around 1695 and lasted until about 1725. In those thirty years, called the Golden Age of Piracy, names like Blackbeard, Calico Jack, and Black Bart came to be known and feared by mariners throughout the region.

After the end of the War of Spanish Succession in 1713, a large number of unemployed English privateers turned pirate and made the Bahama Islands their home base. The Bahamian pirates terrorized merchant shipping throughout the West Indies, in the Gulf of Mexico, and along the East Coast as far north as Maine. They also preyed on ships passing along the Keys, particularly if the vessels were unfortunate enough to wind up on the reef. In 1716, Captain Musson of Carolina was granted authority to hunt for seagoing cutthroats "about Cape Florida [southern tip of Key Biscayne], a station much frequented by pirates."

Bahamian pirates preyed on shipping in the Straits of Florida in the early 1700s (*Harper's Weekly*, Vol. 4, April 14, 1860. From the collections of The Mariners' Museum, Newport News, Virginia)

The Bahamian pirates ruled Nassau until an armed expedition under Governor Woodes Rogers arrived in 1718. Most of the approximately one thousand pirates decided to accept a king's pardon in exchange for giving up a life of piracy, but a few, determined to carry on, were either captured and hanged or driven from the islands.

The second major outbreak of piracy began in 1815 after the end of the Napoleonic Wars and the War of 1812. Thousands of officers and seamen of men-of-war and privateers were suddenly thrown out of work, and many of them gravitated to piracy. At the same time, South and Central American colonies in revolt against Spain were commissioning privateers from any available source to prey on Spanish shipping. Hundreds of unemployed American seamen began sailing under the flags of Buenos Aires, Venezuela, Colombia, and Mexico. Not particularly concerned about the nationality of unarmed merchantmen they came across, many were no better than pirates. An article in a Charleston newspaper in 1816 headlined "Piratical Pirates" commented, "It is a misfortune to the patriots of South America that their flag is abused by a set of desperadoes who aim at nothing but plunder."

Despite numerous legends to the contrary, there is no evidence that there were pirate bases in the Keys. The story of a pirate named Black Caesar operating out of Caesar Creek between Old Rhodes Key and Elliott Key has never been supported by documented facts. Most of the piracies in Keys waters were committed by pirate vessels based in the Bahamas and Cuba. While these pirates stopped in the Keys to take shelter from storms, to obtain water and wood, or to careen and repair their ships, they did not linger long. The Keys natives, when they were still in residence, were not friendly, particularly to non-Spanish speaking mariners. There were no towns in which to sell loot, obtain supplies, and have a good carouse. Add the scarcity of fresh water and the hordes of mosquitoes, and there is little wonder that even the most down-and-out pirates did not set up headquarters in the Florida Keys.

Documented records of piracies in Keys waters are difficult to find. In 1698, a Bahamian pirate named Kelley was reported to have pursued two English ships in the Straits of Florida. In their efforts to escape him, the ships ran aground on one of the Keys and were lost. The crews made their way to Carolina in the ships' boats. The following year, the governor of the Bahamas sent five ships to capture Kelley. Not finding him, they chased an English ship into a harbor in the Keys. The English crew, thinking pirates were pursuing them, fled ashore, preferring to take their chances with the "savage cannibals" of the Keys. The Bahamians brought the English vessel back to New Providence as a prize to be shared with the governor. We can imagine their chagrin when the captain of the English ship miraculously appeared in Nassau and charged them with piracy.

One of the less-bloody piracies took place in the Straits of Florida in 1786. A Spanish snow (similar to a brig), *St. Francisco de Paula,* was on her way from Havana to Spain when she was approached by a ten-gun sloop with a crew of about forty men. The sloop fired a gun and demanded that the snow's captain come over in his boat. Once the captain and his boat crew were aboard the sloop, the pirates confined them to the forward part of the vessel and launched their own boat manned by fourteen cutthroats armed with pistols and cutlasses. When the pirate boarding party reached the *Francisco,* they forced the crew into the bow, cursed them, abused them with threats of bodily harm, and cut one man's hand open with a cutlass. While a guard stood over the snow's crew, the pirates broke open and rifled every trunk and chest onboard. Among these was a consignment of gold and silver worth $33,349. They carried off everything of value they could find, including provisions and live chickens. Finally, at 10:00 P.M., they allowed the captain and his boat crew to return to their ship and then sailed away. The captain said he was unable to determine the pirate crews' nationality, as he heard them speaking English, French, Spanish, and Dutch.

While most of the pirate activity during the second major outbreak (1815–1825) took place in the Gulf of Mexico and the Caribbean, some of it spilled over into the Straits of Florida and the Keys. It was early in this period that one of the few documented cases of pirates making use of a harbor in the Keys occurred.

A Supercargo Slips the Noose

The *Emma Sophia* was a large, square-rigged merchant ship from Hamburg with a cargo of linen and cotton cloth. Her supercargo, the representative of the owner charged with handling all the commercial business of the voyage, was an American named William Savage. In a letter written from Havana in December 1818, Savage described his harrowing experiences at the hands of a band of pirates in the Florida Keys.

On December 19, somewhere between Cay Sal Bank and the Great

Bahama Bank, a small schooner, armed with a single pivot gun and manned by a crew of thirty rogues, came alongside the *Sophia* and ordered her to heave to. A party of twelve armed cutthroats—Spanish, French, German, and American—boarded the *Sophia* and forced the captain to set a course for the lower Florida Keys.

On arriving off the Keys, the pirates directed the *Sophia* to cruise back and forth outside the reef while the schooner sailed in to survey an anchorage. In the morning, the schooner returned, accompanied by two smaller craft, a schooner and a sloop. The *Sophia* followed the three vessels across the reef and anchored in what Savage described as "as snug a hole as buccaneers could wish." Immediately thereafter, a swarm of pirates came aboard, lowered the ships' boats, opened the cargo hatches, and began transferring the *Sophia*'s cargo to their own vessels.

On the afternoon of the next day, the sea-robbers shifted their attention to the crew's personal belongings. They rifled through sea chests, taking anything that caught their fancy, such as packages of laces and gold watches. Brandishing foot-long knives, they threatened to kill every man in the crew if they failed to reveal where their money or other valuables were concealed. For some unknown reason, they directed their most menacing threats at Savage.

Fearing for his life, Savage appealed to the pirates' captain for protection. The captain, a Spaniard who did not look the part of a pirate, took Savage to his schooner, where he told him that he had no control over his crew; they would do whatever they pleased. He advised Savage to tell the pirate crewmen where his money and valuables were concealed and, if he did so, his life would be spared. Savage protested that he had nothing hidden and was sent back to the *Sophia*. That evening, the pirates returned to their craft while the *Sophia*'s crew prayed that they had seen the last of them.

But their prayers were not answered. The next morning, two more pirate craft arrived, and a boat crew from the first schooner again boarded the *Sophia*. They said they had come back to find the gold and other valuables and, if they were not told where they were hidden, they would hang everyone and set the ship on fire.

The leader of the boat crew was an American named Davis. According to Savage, he was the worst of the lot and "the most brutal rascal I ever met." Drawing his knife, Davis swore every man of the crew would die unless they told where their money was hidden, and Savage would be the first to go. Following Davis' order, one of the pirates climbed to the mizzen yard and dropped down a line with a hangman's noose at one end. With one man standing by to hoist, and the other ready to put the noose in place, Davis growled to Savage, "Now, where is the money, where are your diamonds, or I will hang you this minute." Desperately, Savage pleaded that he had nothing more than his watch and offered it to Davis. Scorning the watch, Davis said, "Once more—will you tell?" When Savage protested he had nothing to tell, Davis thundered, "On with the rope and hoist away!"

As the pirate with the noose approached him, Savage sprang to the rail and plunged into the water. The pirates quickly manned a boat and fished Savage out. He feigned unconsciousness as they laid him on the deck and stripped off all his clothes, even the ring from his finger. But then, in a move totally uncharacteristic for pirates, they covered him with a blanket and left him alone. For five hours, Savage lay absolutely still, not daring to move a muscle lest the pirates return to carry out their threat. In the meantime they

Pirate Davis threatened to hang Savage if he did not tell where the money was hidden (redrawn by Wayne Giordano from an illustration by Ray Brown in *The Story of Our Merchant Marine* by Willis J. Abbot, New York: Dodd, Meade and Co., 1919)

busied themselves with robbing the *Sophia*'s crewmen of every possession of any value.

The pirates left the ship that evening, but once or twice during the night, returned to check on Savage's condition. Apparently, despite their threats, they had not actually intended to kill him and now wanted to be sure he lived.

In the morning, three of the pirate vessels departed. The next morning was Christmas morning, and the crew of the *Emma Sophia* awoke to see the best Christmas present they could have asked for—all the pirates were gone. Having carefully observed the courses steered coming in, the captain safely navigated the ship out of the harbor and across the reef. The following morning the *Sophia* moored in Havana harbor.

Savage was of the opinion that the pirates were from Cuba, and that the goods they had stolen, worth about fifty thousand dollars, would be landed there. He concluded his letter with this observation, "The neighborhood of Cuba will be troubled waters until our government shall seriously determine to put down this system of piracy."

More Piracies in the Keys and the Straits

William Savage's prediction was more than correct. Piracies continued to increase, particularly along the Cuban coast. Three months after the *Emma Sophia* incident, Congress authorized the president to send a special naval force to the West Indies to protect American commerce and to capture pirates. The act also authorized merchantmen to arm themselves and encouraged them to resist the pirates with all possible means.

But the Navy ships were too few in number and too large in size to be effective against pirates who operated in small craft hidden in shallow inlets, coves, and rivers. In 1820, pirates robbed twenty-seven American merchantmen and brutalized or murdered their crews. Among them was the schooner *Mary McKoy*. While careened at Tavernier Key, a boat full of cutthroats from a schooner flying the Spanish flag boarded the *McKoy* and robbed her crew. They also robbed three Bahamian wreckers anchored nearby and forced one of the Bahamian captains to pilot the pirate schooner to the harbor at Key West.

By 1822, it was estimated that nearly three thousand piracies had been committed in the seven years since the end of the War of 1812. In January of that year, the American brig *Dover* got under way from Matanzas bound northward through the Straits for Charleston. Five heavily armed Spanish pirates boarded the *Dover* shortly after she left port, beat the crewmen severely, and stole everything of value they could find. The captain later reported, "They then ordered us to stand north [away from the Cuban coast], or they would overhaul us, murder the crew and burn the vessel. We made sail, and shortly after were brought to [stopped] by another boat of the same character, which fired into us, but left us upon being informed that we had been already robbed."

The spring of 1822 continued to be a busy year for pirates operating in the Straits. In April, a ship's captain arriving in Philadelphia from Trinidad reported that several pirates were cruising in the Keys. They had captured a schooner from Boston and marooned the crew on Sand Key. Three of the crewmen perished from lack of water before a passing vessel took them off. It is likely that it was one of these same pirate vessels that stopped and boarded the American brig *Aurilla* in May. After taking off the

Piracy and atrocities grew rapidly following the War of 1812. (*Thrilling Adventures at Sea or Noted Shipwrecks and Famous Sailors,* John W. Lovell Co., circa 1890)

ship's cargo, the pirates used a clever ruse to find out where the ship's and crews' money was concealed. They sent the crew below with a guard, then killed a chicken and dripped its blood over the anchor windlass and some of the cutlasses. They brought a crewman on deck and then concealed him under guard in another part of the vessel. Bringing up another sailor, they surrounded him with drawn cutlasses and demanded he tell where the money was hidden. When the man refused to talk, they told him that the first man had lied and had been killed and tossed overboard. Seeing the blood on the windlass and cutlasses, the sailor confessed all he knew about hidden money. After he was sent below with the first sailor, another was brought up. In the same manner, each crewman was interrogated until the pirates knew where every bit of money onboard was hidden.

Just one month later, a passenger aboard a small schooner that was captured by pirates in "the north entrance to the Straits of Florida" told one of the most blood-curdling tales of pirate sadism ever heard. To force the captain to tell where he had hidden his money, the pirates cut off both his arms at the elbows. After he had revealed the location, they tied him to the deck on a bed of oakum, soaked it with turpentine, stuffed oakum in his mouth, and set him on fire. They hanged another seaman from the yardarm and crucified the boatswain by spiking his feet to the deck and his torso to the tiller. They dispatched the final crewmember by blowing his head off with the swivel gun. Even the ship's dog was not spared: They shot him twice and then cut out his tongue. The passenger, bound tightly to the foremast, watched the macabre scene unfold in horror. The pirates then returned to their vessel, leaving the schooner slowly filling with water and the still-bound passenger to his fate. But before the schooner sank, a passing ship sighted her and rescued the passenger.

In March 1822, Congress authorized an increase in the West India Squadron to fourteen ships. Despite some captures, piracies and atrocities continued to occur, particularly along the Cuban coast.

Death of a Pirate Fighter

Among the ships of the West India Squadron was the U.S. Schooner *Alligator*, one of four topsail schooners built for the Navy in 1820 and 1821,

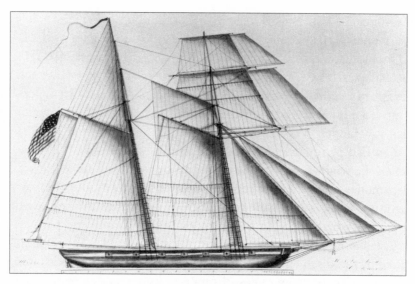

United States Schooner *Alligator* (courtesy of National Archives)

specially designed to hunt slavers and pirates. She was eighty-six feet long, armed with twelve guns, and a fast sailer with a huge spread of canvas. In November 1822, under the command of Lt. William H. Allen USN, the *Alligator* was on patrol off the north coast of Cuba with a crew of nine officers and forty-five seamen and marines.

On November 8, the *Alligator* sailed into the harbor at Matanzas, where three American merchantmen had been captured by pirates the year before. As she was anchoring, the master of an American brig and the mate of an American schooner came aboard. They informed Allen that their vessels had been captured by pirates and were lying in a bay about thirty miles to the east. The pirates had sent the captain and mate to Matanzas to obtain a ransom of seven thousand dollars for the release of their ships and their crews. If they were not back in three days with the money, the pirates swore they would burn the ships and every soul onboard. The two men were in the process, with the help of merchants of the port, of outfitting a small schooner, the *Ploughboy,* to try to retake their vessels.

Allen immediately ordered sail set and headed east, accompanied by the *Ploughboy.* Upon arriving at the entrance to the bay early the following morning, he sighted the masts of several vessels behind some small islands.

The American merchant captain identified one of them, a schooner under sail, as one of the pirates.

The water was too shallow to proceed further, so Allen ordered his crew to let go the anchor and lower the three boats. Allen took command of the launch, accompanied by a marine captain, the American merchant captain, and thirteen seamen and marines. Lieutenant Dale (*Alligator*'s second-in-command), the American mate, and ten men went in the cutter, and Midshipman Henley and four men manned the gig. The combined force of thirty-three officers and men began rowing toward the pirate schooner. The *Ploughboy,* under Acting Lieutenant Cunningham with two midshipmen and twenty men, followed but was soon left behind because of a lack of wind.

Because the wind was so light, the pirate schooner began using her sweeps (long oars) to escape, but after a chase of two hours covering a distance of ten miles, the *Alligator*'s boats pulled within gunshot range. The name *Revenge* was carved on the pirate ship's stern, and her deck was crowded with about thirty cutthroats. As the boat crews prepared to board, the schooner turned, hoisted a red flag, and fired a broadside of round and grape shot. But the aim was wild and there was no damage to the boats. Allen immediately maneuvered his three boats to regain a position astern of the schooner. In the meantime, a second pirate schooner with about sixty rogues onboard arrived on the scene and began firing at the boats.

Accurate musket fire by the *Alligator*'s marines began taking a toll on the *Revenge* and soon drove the pirates away from their guns. Twice they jumped into boats they had been towing alongside and attempted to reach their consort. The first time, the *Alligator*'s boats headed them off and they returned onboard. The second time, just as the *Alligator*'s boats reached a position to board, the pirates made good their escape and joined their fellow cutthroats on the second schooner.

Leaving Midshipman Henley and his four seamen to take charge of the *Revenge,* Allen headed the launch and the cutter toward the second schooner. Now the odds were ninety pirates to twenty-eight Navy men. Allen, already wounded once, stood up in the launch to encourage his men and to direct the attack. A second musket ball thudded into his chest. Ignoring his wounds, he continued to urge his men forward. As the boats drew closer, the pirates' musket fire became more effective, killing two seamen and severely wounding four others. With the dead and wounded slumped over their oars, both boats became unmanageable and fell back.

Despite their overwhelming numerical superiority, the pirates, many of them lying wounded on deck among others who were dead, had no stomach to continue the fight. They headed their schooner inshore, where they were joined by a third pirate schooner more heavily armed than the first two. The action, which had lasted only a half hour, was over. The unwounded men in the launch and cutter rowed alongside the *Revenge* and carefully lifted their wounded captain and shipmates aboard.

Lieutenant Allen died about four hours later, along with one of the wounded seamen. Until his death, Allen continued to give orders and to converse cheerfully with his men. The surgeon reported that "he wished his relatives and his country to know that he had fought well, and added that he died in peace and good will toward all the world, and hoped for his reward in the next."

In the afternoon and again on the following morning, the *Alligator's* boats rowed into the bay and recovered the five American vessels that the pirates had abandoned. Under the command of Lieutenant Dale, the *Alligator* with her prize, the *Revenge,* and the five American merchant vessels returned to Matanzas, where Lieutenant Allen was buried with full military honors. While still in Matanzas, Dale learned through the local grapevine that the *Alligator's* boat crews had killed fifteen pirates, including their second-in-command, and wounded many more.

Loss of the Alligator

Nine days after the battle with the pirates, the *Alligator* got under way for Norfolk under the command of Lieutenant Dale. Her prize, the pirate schooner *Revenge,* and a convoy of American merchantmen sailed with her for protection during their passage through the pirate-infested waters along the Cuban coast and in the Straits of Florida.

After clearing Matanzas Bay, Dale set a course slightly east of north. This course would take the convoy well clear of Cay Sal Bank to the west and into the "Gulph," as navigators then called the Straits of Florida. The Florida Current would then carry them northward, parallel to—but well clear of—the Keys and the treacherous reef. As the day wore on, one of the convoy ships, the brig *Ann Maria,* began to fall astern and off to the west. Dale was concerned for her safety. Before leaving Matanzas, he had received intelligence that the pirates were planning to pick off stragglers from the convoy. He altered course to keep the brig in sight and during the night made short tacks to slow his advance and stay with the convoy.

In the morning, *Alligator's* lookouts could see only two ships of the convoy, and by 4:00 in the afternoon, only the *Ann Maria,* now even further to the west, could be seen. Believing the rest of the convoy to be even further to the west, Dale altered course to the north and then to the west of north to try to regain visual contact.

As a dark, hazy night fell, the midshipman on watch ordered three lookouts stationed—one at the bow, one on the fore yard, and one at the stern. He also made sure that the leadsman took a sounding with the deep-sea lead every half hour. As a further precaution, he compared the temperatures of the water and air every hour. If the water temperature began to drop, it would indicate that the ship was straying out of the Florida Current into the cooler near-shore waters.

At 9:00 P.M., the leadsman reported no bottom at forty-five fathoms (270 feet). The temperature of the water and air were both seventy-nine degrees, and the *Alligator* was clipping along at five knots under a fresh, easterly breeze. Thirty minutes later, a violent shock shook the ship as she ground her way onto the reef and then came to a sickening stop. Dale ran up on deck and ordered the sails furled and the boats hoisted out. From soundings taken around the ship, the boats' crews determined that the closest deep water was astern. Seamen on deck lowered a kedge anchor to the longboat, and her crew rowed out to deep water and released it. The men onboard heaved around with the capstan trying to drag the *Alligator* astern, but before she would move, the anchor line parted.

It was obvious that the ship had to be lightened before there was any chance she could be hauled free. Dale ordered the crew to heave all the cannon and shot overboard with the exception of two carronades. For the rest of the night and into the next day, crewmen continued jettisoning heavy items such as anchor chains, ballast stones, spare sails, and yards. In the meantime, the wind veered to the southeast, freshened, and drove the *Alligator* further onto the reef.

At first light, the longboat's crew carried out the best bower (starboard bow anchor) and dropped it well astern in deep water. At high tide, the capstan gang heaved around but only succeeded in dragging the anchor back to the ship. Any further attempts to kedge her off appeared to be hopeless because of the poor holding ground. At the next high tide, the captain ordered all sails set in hopes of driving her across the reef into Hawk Channel, but she remained fast aground.

On the morning of the second day on the reef, a schooner approached and hove to nearby. The *Alligator's* boat crew rowed over and learned that she was a wrecker from New Providence. Dale engaged the wrecker to stand by, and he transferred valuable items such as ship's papers and money to her by boat. A short while later, another sail was sighted to the west. The captain ordered the carronades fired to attract her attention and sent a boat to meet her. She proved to be the wayward brig *Ann Maria*. By this time, Dale knew that his ship was lost. The brig came as close as she dared, and the *Alligator's* boats began transferring to her anything of value that had not been thrown overboard. Dale remained aboard his ship that final night as the seas rolled in and pounded her on the reef, expecting at any moment to find her breaking up beneath him.

In the morning, after his crew had been transferred to the brig, Dale and several of his men set fire to their ship to prevent her from falling into the hands of pirates. At 4:00 she blew up, and the *Ann Maria* set sail for Norfolk.

On arriving, Dale presented a letter to the senior officer present requesting a court of inquiry into the loss of his ship. After hearing testimony from the schooner's officers and from Dale, the court delivered its opinion that the loss of the *Alligator* was due to the frequent changes of course made to keep company with the convoy, an unusual counter current, and the darkness and haziness of the night. The court found no fault with the actions of the officers and crew and praised the efforts of Lieutenant Dale, his officers, and his men in trying to save their ship.

Today, the Alligator Reef lighthouse off Upper Matecumbe Key marks the approximate location of the loss of a gallant pirate-fighting ship.

The Antipiracy Squadron Avenges Lieutenant Allen

The death of Lieutenant Allen and his men received wide publicity and outraged the public. Congress quickly appropriated funds to further expand the West India (Antipiracy) Squadron. Capt. David Porter, naval hero of the War of 1812 and a man of action, was placed in command with orders to establish his headquarters at Key West, which he named Thompson's Island after the secretary of the Navy. As the commander of a squadron, Porter was accorded the courtesy title of commodore and was generally referred to as Commodore Porter even after he no longer held that command.

In order to catch the small pirate craft that generally operated in shallow coastal waters, Porter purchased eight shoal-draft, fast-sailing Chesapeake Bay schooners. Appropriately named *Fox, Greyhound, Jackall, Beagle, Terrier, Weasel, Wild Cat,* and *Ferret,* each was armed with three guns and manned by a crew of thirty-one officers and men. To follow the pirates into even shallower coves, inlets, and rivers, he obtained five twenty-oared gun barges and named them *Mosquito, Gnat, Midge, Sandfly,* and *Gallinipper.* But the most unusual addition to his command was a steam-driven, side-wheel ferryboat that could be used to tow the barges. The *Sea Gull,* as Porter named her, was armed with three guns and became the first steam vessel in the world to see active naval service. Because the small craft of the squadron

Commodore Porter's Antipiracy Squadron at Key West (copied by Mariners' Museum from *Memoir of Commodore Porter of the U.S. Navy,* J. Munsell, 1875. From the collections of The Mariners' Museum, Newport News, Virginia)

carried a biting sting and operated close inshore under constant bombardment by hordes of insects, they came to be known as the Mosquito Fleet.

After a reconnaissance voyage through the Caribbean, stopping at Puerto Rico, Santo Domingo, and Cuba, Porter's squadron arrived at Key West in April 1823. In his usual imperious manner, Porter took over the island as if it were another unit of his command, landed the marines, and began construction of storehouses, living quarters, and a hospital. In honor of the memory of Lieutenant Allen, he named the naval depot Allenton.

Porter spread the squadron's forces throughout the Caribbean wherever there were reports of pirate activity. The larger ships convoyed American merchantmen through the most dangerous waters and patrolled off ports suspected of harboring pirates. The smaller craft hunted along the coasts, particularly those of Cuba, looking into every cove, inlet, or river that might hide a nest of pirates. It was the most arduous and debilitating duty imaginable. For weeks on end, the sailors and marines lived in open boats packed full with provisions, water, ammunition, and arms, as well as their limited personal gear. There was no protection from the burning tropical sun or wind-blown spray. At night they pulled their boats up onshore and slept on the ground, tormented by hordes of mosquitoes and sandflies. They were in constant danger of being ambushed by pirates or unfriendly natives or, far worse, of contracting yellow fever. The fatality rate for yellow fever was sixty percent—many more men died from fever than from pirate's bullets.

In May, Porter had directed Lt. William H. Watson, captain of the *Sea Gull,* to take the barges *Gallinipper* and *Mosquito* in tow and to scout the Cuban coast along the Old Bahama Channel as far as Matanzas. It was now nearly the middle of July, and perspiration soaked Porter's shirt as he paced the quarterdeck of his flagship anchored in Key West harbor. Based on letters he wrote, his thoughts might have run like this:

We should have heard something from Watson by now. If only he has managed to lay some of those cutthroats by the heels, what a boost it would be to the squadron's morale. Piracy is way down since we arrived, but those damn Northern newspapers are still on my back because we haven't hung any of the rogues yet. Their editors just don't understand that all the pirates have to do is say they are poor fishermen, show us a Spanish passport, and, unless we catch them in the act, they go free.

I had no use for this place when I arrived three months ago. I even wrote that the lack of fresh water would prevent it from ever becoming a permanent naval base and God forbid it should, for it is occupation enough to keep one's self free of the mosquitoes and sandflies. But I am beginning to change my mind. This island has enormous strategic advantages. It is of little consequence who possesses Cuba; if we keep a force here we have complete command of the Gulf of Mexico, all the commerce of which, as well as that from Jamaica and Cuba, is completely at our mercy. It is almost incredible, the number of vessels that daily pass and repass this island. I had no concept of the extent of our trade in this area until I came here. I am now fully persuaded that this is the proper place from whence to give it protection.

At this moment, the officer of the watch approached with rapid steps, touched his hat, and reported, "Sir, we have smoke in sight on the horizon!" Porter raised a telescope to his eye and, after a brief search, said, "Yes, that's the *Sea Gull*. I can make out her tall stack and the tops of her big sidewheels.

United States Steam Galliot *Sea Gull*, first steam vessel to see active naval service. Lt. Watson was captain in 1823 (courtesy of Monroe County Public Library)

Signal Lieutenant Watson to report to me as soon as he is anchored."

Two hours later, Watson climbed up the side of the flagship and was piped aboard. Porter, impatient for his report, was waiting topside. "What news do you bring us, Mr. Watson?"

The lieutenant, standing stiffly at attention, swept off his hat and said, "Sir, I have the honor to report the capture of the pirate schooner *Catalina* and the near total elimination of her crew of some seventy or eighty pirates. The action took place on the fifth of July in Siguapa Bay, the very same bay in which Lieutenant Allen met his untimely fate. I take great satisfaction in being able to report that his death has been avenged."

"Well done, Watson, very well done!" Porter exclaimed. "Come below. I'll assemble my staff, and you can tell us the full story."

A short while later, seated in the commodore's cabin, Lieutenant Watson began.

I left the *Sea Gull* to continue her patrol in Old Bahama Channel while I proceeded to the west to explore the keys and bays along the coast with the two barges. I was in the *Gallinipper* with thirteen men, and Lieutenant Inman was in the *Mosquito* with ten, which was all the hands we could spare from the *Sea Gull*. When we reached Siguapa Bay, about thirteen leagues to windward of Matanzas, we sighted a large topsail schooner with a launch in company beating up toward several merchant vessels at anchor. I immediately headed toward her to investigate and signaled *Gallinipper* to follow.

When we were within gun-shot range, I could see that the schooner had several large guns and her deck was filled with men. I hoisted our colors and the schooner hoisted a Spanish flag. No sooner had the flag been raised than she brailed up [partially furled] her foresail, fired her guns at us, and then hauled down the Spanish flag. Their shots went wide, and I changed course to approach from their quarter, signaling Inman to do the same. But the schooner turned to run before the wind and, being faster than us, pulled away and headed toward the shore.

Upon reaching the vicinity of a small village, the pirates anchored and put springs on their anchor cable so they could swing ship to bring their guns to bear on us. When we were about thirty yards away, they

Lts. Watson and Inman in barges *Gallinipper* and *Mosquito* attacking
pirates on the Cuban coast (watercolor by Irwin J. Bevan, Bailey Collection.
From the collections of The Mariners' Museum, Newport News, Virginia)

fired a volley with their muskets, but their aim was wild, and, incredibly, not a single one of our men was hit.

As we moved in to board, my men gave three cheers and fired their
muskets. In a panic, the cowardly cutthroats leaped overboard, some
into the launch and others into the water, heading for the shore. We
fired another volley at the launch and they abandoned her also. By rowing rapidly, we were able to get between the pirates and shore. Our men
began shouting 'Allen, Allen, remember Allen!' as they shot and
stabbed the swimmers. After a few minutes of this carnage, I gave the
order to grant quarter, but the men had gone wild and could not be
restrained.

We counted twenty-seven dead, but as a number of the bodies sank,
I think we dispatched at least thirty or thirty-five. A few of them made
it to shore, but our sailors and marines landed and pursued them,
killing seven and severely wounding and capturing another five. Four
more were caught by the local authorities, but unfortunately, so I was
told, their leader, the infamous Diaboleta [Little Devil], escaped.

The pirate schooner, which I have brought with me as prize, was armed with one long nine-pounder and two six-pounders. Had any of their shots hit, we would have sunk immediately. I am gratified to inform you, sir, that not a single one of my men was wounded.

"Splendid work, Watson," Porter exclaimed. "This news will take the wind out of those Northern editors' sails. When I think of the odds against you, more than three to one, and the armament you faced, I must say that bringing your men away without a scratch is nothing short of miraculous. Let us drink a toast to your victory, to the memory of Lieutenant Allen, and damnation to the pirates!"

In a general order to the squadron, Commodore Porter praised the gallantry of Lieutenant Watson and his men. From among the captured arms, each officer was awarded a sword, each petty officer a pistol, and each seaman or marine a musket. Porter recommended Watson for promotion, but just two months later, the squadron's worst enemy, yellow fever, claimed him.

Commodore Porter Versus the Proprietors of Key West

During the three years that Commodore Porter commanded the antipiracy squadron, he spent only ten months at Key West, largely because of yellow fever epidemics. For the rest of the time, he directed the operations of his squadron from sea or from Washington. By the end of the three years, he had succeeded not only in ridding the Caribbean of nearly all pirates but also in arousing the undying enmity of the proprietors (property owners) of Key West.

As captain of the *Essex* in the War of 1812, Porter captured the first British warship, decimated the British whaling fleet in the Pacific, and fought a gallant but losing battle against two British warships when he was blockaded at Valparaiso. While he was a brilliant naval leader, he was also inclined to be short-tempered, impetuous, and arrogant.

When Porter first arrived at Key West, the island was occupied by John Whitehead and John Fleeming, each of whom had purchased a one-quarter share of the island from John Simonton. There were also a small number of settlers, most of whom worked for the island's proprietors.

It was largely through the efforts of Simonton that the Navy became aware of Key West and its advantages as a base for the war against the pirates. The proprietors expected the arrival of the Navy to be a boon to their plans for developing the island into a major seaport and a center for salvaging cargoes from wrecked ships. In anticipation of the Navy's arrival, they had three hundred cords of stove wood cut and ready for sale and had imported a large number of sheep and hogs to supply fresh meat to the sailors. The animals were allowed to roam free to fatten up on the island's vegetation. The proprietors had also developed a plan for the town's layout and had built a warehouse and several houses.

Cordial at first, relations between Porter and the owners deteriorated rapidly when Porter's sailors began carrying off the stove wood and shooting the sheep and hogs without payment. The proprietors showed their plans for the town to Porter, expecting that he would take them into consideration in selecting sites for building. But his carpenters paid no attention to the civilians' plans: They built the Navy's storehouses and workshops on choice waterfront lots that the proprietors had reserved for themselves. Porter soon made it evident that because ownership of the island was in dispute between Simonton and another purchaser, he considered the entire island to be U.S. government property. On this basis, he dictated where and what the property owners could build and even gave permission to others to build on their lots without recompense.

Porter's initial low opinion of Key West as a naval station was not improved when, in August, a severe epidemic of yellow fever broke out. Porter himself, for the third time in his life, was one of the victims. After forty-eight of his officers and men had died, he ordered most of the squadron to head north, leaving only a skeleton force on the island. The officer-in-charge during Porter's absence continued his commander's autocratic rule. He ordered the arrest of John Mallory for selling a pint of cider to a sailor. Despite the fact that Mallory was at home in bed undergoing medical treatment, the officer's men dragged him to the guard house. Mallory protested that he had the commodore's permission to sell not only cider, but ale, porter, and wine as well. In reply, the officer told him he could pay a fine of twenty dollars or be flogged with thirty-nine lashes. Mallory, seeing he had no recourse, paid the fine and was released the next day.

Porter returned to Key West with his family in April 1824. Within two months, he again came down with yellow fever and, with his family, returned to Washington. This time, he left Lieutenant McIntosh in charge of the island. Busy as Porter was with running the war against the pirates, he did not neglect to oversee affairs at Key West. Replying to a letter from McIntosh about the arrival of some women who were ill, Porter reiterated his policies. Despite the fact that ownership of the island had, by this time, been settled in favor of Simonton, Porter said, "I consider the island as in the hands or occupancy of the United States . . . I considered them [civilians], in fact, as merely tolerated on the island, so long as they may submit to the rules which I may prescribe for their government." He also told McIntosh not to permit any more settlers on the island without his permission and to inform owners that any livestock not confined to pens would be considered to be the property of the government. Of course, the latter edict was no news to the owners.

The secretary of the Navy, more than a little perturbed that Porter had left his station without permission, ordered him to return. Porter, equally perturbed with the secretary, requested to be relieved of his command but complied with the order. On his way back to Key West, he landed a force of two hundred sailors and marines at Foxardo, Puerto Rico, to demand an apology from the mayor for the arrest of an American naval officer (who was in civilian clothes at the time).

Arriving in Key West for the third and last time (as a U.S. Navy officer), Porter once again locked horns with one of the proprietors. This time, it was Pardon C. Greene, a merchant, who now owned a one-quarter share of the island. Greene had been appointed by John Whitehead, the only civil authority on the island, as agent for the sale of cargo from a French brig that had been captured through the combined efforts of two naval warships, one American, the other British. When Porter learned that Greene expected to take a customary five percent agent's fee on the sale, he forbade him to act as agent for the U.S. Navy share of the cargo. Whitehead protested that Porter was overriding his authority, to no avail.

In February 1825, Captain Warrington arrived in Key West and relieved Porter of command of the West India Squadron. In the fall of that year, following another outbreak of yellow fever, the Navy ordered

Warrington to move the base to Pensacola. When Porter returned north to face a court of inquiry, the property owners and merchants of Key West rejoiced. The court recommended he be court-martialed for his insult to the local Spanish government at Foxardo and for insubordinate conduct and conduct unbecoming an officer in letters he wrote to the president and to the secretary of the Navy. The court-martial board found him guilty and sentenced him to six months' suspension from duty. In 1826, Porter resigned from the U.S. Navy to accept a commission as commander of the Mexican Navy.

Twenty-two years later, Simonton and the other proprietors addressed a memorial to Congress detailing the many injustices and injuries of Porter's autocratic rule and the resulting loss of revenue, which they put at not less than two to three hundred thousand dollars. The Committee for Naval Affairs agreed that their statements and complaints were well founded and stated in a report, "The government had no right to take the property of the petitioners for public use without making to them a suitable compensation." However, despite the favorable report, no compensation was ever made.

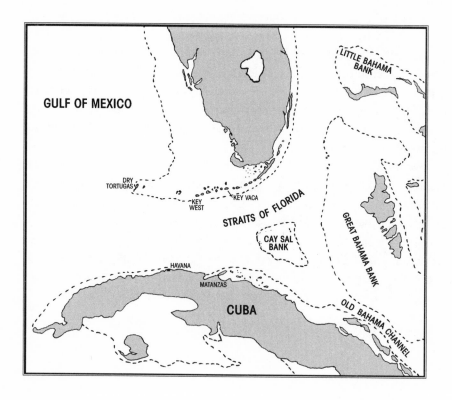

Chapter 5

MEXICAN INTERLOPERS

Arrival of Mexican Squadron in Key West

*T*he thirty-six-gun frigate *Libertad,* flagship of the Mexican Squadron under the command of former U.S. Navy Captain David Porter, followed by the fourteen-gun brig *Bravo,* dropped anchor in Key West harbor on December 26, 1826. Two days later, the eighteen-gun brig *Victoria* and the five-gun schooner *Hermon* sailed in to join the squadron.

Mexico and Spain were at war over Spain's attempts to regain control of her former Mexican colony. While the U.S. government was sympathetic to the Mexican cause, it was officially neutral. For the next nine months, the Mexican men-of-war under Porter's command used Key West as a base for raids against Spanish shipping and as a haven for protection against a superior Spanish squadron lying offshore. Never before or since has U.S. neutrality been so blatantly violated.

Key West settlers did not greet Porter's return to the island with any great enthusiasm. Two years earlier, when he had been relieved of command of the antipiracy squadron and ordered north to face a court martial, the residents had been more than happy to see the end of his autocratic rule.

After his resignation from the U.S. Navy over what he considered a totally unjustified verdict and sentence of the court martial, Porter accepted an offer from the Mexican government to take command of its tiny, inef-

Captain David Porter, Commander-in-Chief of the
Mexican Navy (courtesy of Monroe County Public Library)

fectual Navy. Together with two of his sons, David Dixon, age twelve, and Thomas, age ten, Porter arrived in Vera Cruz in May 1826. For the next seven months, he labored to put the Mexican ships in fighting trim and to instill discipline in their officers and men. In early December, he took his four-ship squadron to sea. Cruising off Matanzas, Cuba, for three weeks, he captured two Spanish merchantmen. Then, on Christmas day, he sighted two Spanish frigates headed toward him. Knowing they had greatly superior firepower, he set course for the Keys and escaped under cover of a storm. The Spanish guessed his destination and quickly stationed a powerful blockading force off Key West.

Porter claimed that since his squadron was blockaded, he was entitled under international law to the sanctuary of a neutral port, and he settled down to play cat and mouse with the Spanish ships. With detailed knowledge of Keys waters gained during his three years in command of the antipiracy squadron, Porter was able to give his captains directions on how to evade the blockade. They left port and returned with captured ships without being intercepted by the blockading forces.

There was no one in Key West to contest the Mexican Squadron's occupation. The Navy, because of yellow fever outbreaks, had abandoned Key West and moved to Pensacola. The only civil authority on the island was the collector of the port, William Pinckney. Whereas Porter had many

Key West in 1826 (drawing by Titian Ramsay Peale, collection of the American Philosophical Society, courtesy of Monroe County Public Library)

enemies among the merchants, Pinckney was a true and needed friend. Pinckney was a nephew of the U.S. Navy's senior officer, Commodore John Rodgers, and Porter probably already knew him. Throughout Porter's stay at Key West, Pinckney defended him and asserted that he was not violating U.S. neutrality. In light of the Mexican Squadron's operations, it is impossible to understand how he could justify such a position.

During Porter's first six months at Key West, the Mexican ships captured twenty-one Spanish vessels, one of them worth $150,000. In addition, they destroyed many smaller craft and brought Cuban coastal trade to a halt. And Porter's raiders did not confine their operations to the sea. As one officer wrote, "We march into the country and play them all sorts of pranks." In one of these pranks, a Mexican landing force went ashore a few miles from Havana and captured a mule train carrying coffee.

The Cruise of the Esmeralda

Commodore Porter, wishing his sons to follow in his footsteps, appointed both of them midshipmen in the Mexican Navy. David Dixon Porter, who was to achieve fame as a Union naval officer in the Civil War and who would later become Admiral of the Navy, had just turned thirteen when his father assigned him to duty aboard the captured schooner *Esmeralda*. The schooner's captain, Lt. David H. Porter, was young David's cousin. The remainder of the crew consisted of an English carpenter named Barret, an old Swedish quartermaster named Simms, an English cabin boy, two Americans, and twenty-three Mexicans.

The *Esmeralda* slipped through the Spanish blockade with the simple ruse of a crudely made American flag and made her way around the western tip of Cuba. On deck she carried a fourteen-oared barge. Under cover of darkness, the Mexican sailors rowed the barge into harbors along the Cuban coast and captured several small schooners. After sending the Cuban crewmen ashore, the barge crew transferred their cargoes to the *Esmeralda* and burned or sank the vessels.

Lieutenant Porter was a harsh disciplinarian and did not spare the use of the cat-o'-nine-tails. When a landing party went on a looting spree against his express orders, he had every man in the party flogged. David Dixon noted that Barret, who had been flogged a number of times for being drunk, was moving among the Mexican sailors and talking to them in a surreptitious manner. His suspicions aroused, David went to the cabin and discovered that two muskets, several cutlasses, and all the bayonets he had issued to the landing party were missing. Then the cabin boy told David that he had overheard one of the Mexicans say that the *Esmeralda* would have a new captain in twenty-four hours.

David sent the cabin boy to tell the captain what he had discovered while he stayed behind to guard the weapons. The captain hurried to the cabin, took a position outside the door, and, with Simms at his side, called the crew to quarters. When Barret appeared on the bow along with the Mexican seamen, Porter roared, "Barret, lay aft, you drunken scoundrel! "

"I'm no more a drunken scoundrel than you!" Barret yelled back. Shouting to the Mexicans to follow him, Barret ran at the captain with an ax. Young David handed the captain a pistol and passed a cutlass to Simms. The old Swede cut down Barret, and the captain shot down the leading Mexican. The mutineers retreated as Simms ran into the cowed group and knocked several down with his fists.

While the captain held the men at bay with cocked pistols, David and Simms fastened irons on their wrists and removed the bayonets they found hidden in their shirts. But now there were only six men to handle the schooner and still keep guard on twenty-three prisoners. The captain solved the problem in a unique manner: He had twenty-three pairs of holes cut in the cabin roof, put the prisoners' feet into the holes, and chained them together.

The short-handed crew sailed the *Esmeralda* safely back through the blockade and into Key West. The mutineers were placed in boats, flogged alongside each ship in the squadron, and sent back to hard labor in Mexico. This was young David Dixon's first taste of action with the Mexican Navy but by no means his last.

Lieutenant Thompson's Raid and Capture

One of the elder Porter's favorite ruses was to arm and man a captured Spanish merchant vessel and send it out as a commerce raider. Of course, this was in direct violation of U.S. neutrality, but Porter was able to get away with it because of U.S. sympathy with the Mexican cause and because, as a naval hero of the War of 1812, he had many friends in high government positions.

Lt. Alexander Thompson, a former U.S. Navy midshipman, was one of a number of U.S. naval personnel who had followed Porter's footsteps into the Mexican Navy in search of adventure and prize money. Thompson got his chance for both when Porter sent him on a commerce raiding cruise as captain of a captured Spanish schooner. The story of Thompson's adventures is best told in his own words.

I took an old rotten schooner . . . and at Key West put on board of her 20 days' provisions, hoisted the ship's first cutter into her, a fourteen oared boat, took the boat's crew, four soldiers, and one midshipman with me, and sailed on the 15th of March [1827], at night, for the old Bahama Straights [Old Bahama Channel between northeast coast of Cuba and edge of Great Bahama Bank]. It happened that the wind left

In an old schooner, Lt. Thompson captured five Spanish merchant vessels along the Cuban coast (redrawn by Wayne Giordano from an illustration in *Harper's Monthly*, February, 1895)

me, and in the morning, I found myself among the enemies' squadron [Spanish blockaders off Key West]; they however took no notice of my old schooner, and I followed on my business. Two days out I took two prizes and destroyed them, and being the Equinox, I had all the elements to contend with; a heavy North Wester caught me, and almost ruined my old craft; however with much difficulty I got to a safe anchorage, where I knew that with any good weather I could soon get a better vessel. I captured one and chased another, but in the heavy weather she escaped into the port of Remedios [Cuba], and before she could bring the Philistines upon me, I was off with the boat, vessel and prize to another part of the coast, where I captured another schooner; and having gained intelligence of more, proceeded immediately 15 miles in my boat, and after pulling against wind and tide all night, at day-light boarded and cut out two large schooners, brought them down the river Sagua to the place I left; I then had a squadron of five schooners besides my boat, and found myself with thirty-three prisoners. I gave ten their liberty and a small schooner; put seven of my men on board the other two most valuable prizes, hoisted my boat on board another one, and took the remaining twenty-three prisoners with me, burnt my old schooner, and went to sea by the light of her, bound to Key West.

Another spell of bad weather separated me from my prize, but I got inside the Florida Reef, and safe from enemies, and with a pilot on board, who, by the by, was a fool and would not run in the night. He anchored me among rocks, my cabel [anchor cable] chafed off, another cursed gale came on, the tide against me, and I was forced to run onshore. I got out my boat, put in all the prisoners, put five men well armed in the stern sheets, and the prisoners at the oars, and determined to row to Key West. It came on squally, and the rain fell in torrents, so as to wet our fire arms, and nearly filled the boat with water. We had neared the frigate [Porter's flagship, the *Libertad,* anchored at Key West] to within a few miles, and I felt little fear of the prisoners, when about midnight, as I was attending to bailing the boat, four or five set on me; an instant rising was the consequence; the priming of my men's pistols refused fire. I was wounded slightly in the face, and we were instantly secured—23 against 6.

They immediately went back to the prize schooner aground, made the pilot answer the hail, got on board of her by treachery, and secured the midshipman, four soldiers and two sailors I had left with him. The weather soon became fine, and they were enabled to get off and bring us into this place [Havana], where we arrived yesterday. I was blameable in this—trusting so many prisoners to so small a guard; but if I had not encountered the worst weather that ever mortal was afflicted with, there would have been no danger. I am treated with all kindness, politeness and respect, by the Spanish officers . . . I think it will not be long before I am again on board the *Libertad.*

Better that Key West Was Shoveled into the Sea

The commodore of the West India Squadron at Pensacola was directed to check on the situation at Key West periodically but was not given any authority to seize the commerce raiders or to kick Porter out. One of the squadron's visits to Key West was led by Porter's former flagship, the *John Adams,* accompanied by two other U.S. Navy ships. Many of the men in the Mexican squadron were former U.S. Navy sailors and veterans of the antipiracy squadron. When the former shipmates got together again in Key West, there was much drinking and celebration of old times. The Mexican-American sailors urged their former comrades to join them for better pay and adventure. The commander of the U.S. squadron decided to cut the visit short before he lost half his men to the Mexican Navy.

Not everyone was as sympathetic to Porter's operations as Washington was. Porter was selling the cargoes of his prizes, particularly large quantities of coffee, sugar, and tobacco, in Key West. The local merchants protested to Washington that he was ruining their business. The editors of *Niles Register* were equally upset. They wrote:

Key West, we are variously informed, has been made a grand depot for smugglers; and by com. Porter is rendered a place of *rendezvous* for carrying on a predatory and inglorious war against the coasters of Cuba. This must not be permitted. . . . We cannot allow any foreigner to involve us in his quarrel. . . . We are at peace with the people of Cuba, and they are among our best customers . . . if their captain-general shall shut his ports in retaliation of these aggressions, as it has been suggested that he may, what shall we think of it? It would be better for us that Key West was *shovelled* into the sea. Let com. Porter seek the open ocean, and there do what the law of nations permits to *his* enemy—but not shelter himself under the flag which he has abandoned, to depredate on the property of the Spanish subjects.

Porter Commissions a Privateer and Narrowly Escapes

The Spanish government, its commerce with Cuba almost at a standstill, protested that Porter was violating U.S. neutrality. Key West merchants, their business ruined by the sale of cargoes from captured Spanish ships, complained bitterly to their representatives in Washington. The commander of the U.S. Navy squadron at Pensacola warned Washington that Porter had forty blank commissions for privateers which, if used to commission that many privateers, would pose a serious threat to American commerce with Cuba.

Just as the president's orders forbidding Porter from engaging in any further commerce raiding were being issued, a Colombian privateer, the *Caraboba,* sailed into Key West. Her captain, Charles Hopner, a former American citizen, was no stranger to Porter. Four years earlier, when he was in command of the antipiracy squadron at Key West, Porter learned that Hopner, then in command of the Colombian privateer *La Centilla,* was deliberately wrecking his prizes on remote Florida Keys. He would sell their cargoes to Joshua Appleby, proprietor of a small wreckers' settlement on Key Vaca. This was a violation of international law and an evasion of customs duties. Porter sent a sloop-of-war to arrest Appleby and intercept *La Centilla,* but the privateer escaped. Porter then attacked Hopner in the press, accusing him of criminal activities. Hopner denied the charges and reminded Porter that he had often protected American merchant ships from pirates and had even assisted a U.S. Navy brig-of-war in capturing a large band of pirates.

When Hopner sailed the *Caraboba* into Key West in June of 1827, Porter conveniently underwent a change of heart and welcomed him as an ally. Hopner told Porter that his Colombian privateer's commission was about to expire and he had heard that Porter had Mexican commissions available. Well aware of Hopner's success as a commerce raider, Porter was only too happy to oblige him. To avoid further accusations of violating U.S. neutrality, Porter proposed that Hopner meet him three miles offshore to accept the commission. The *Caraboba* got under way, followed by the Mexican schooner-of-war *Bravo* with Porter onboard. After receiving his commission, Hopner hoisted the Mexican colors and renamed his schooner the *Molestador*.

Just as the meeting was ending, lookouts reported sighting the Spanish blockading force of two frigates and a brig coming over the horizon under full sail. With their return to Key West blocked, Porter and Hopner headed their ships up the Keys. For two days, the Spanish chased the *Bravo* and the *Molestador* along the reef. But with their superior knowledge of Keys waters and the shallower drafts of their vessels, Porter and Hopner were able to escape. Porter returned to Key West while Hopner headed toward Cuba. In a matter of days, Hopner destroyed seven Spanish fishing vessels and captured a merchant ship. Returning to Key West with his prize, he transferred his prisoners to Porter's flagship and headed across the Atlantic to raid commerce along the coast of Spain.

The Mexican Squadron Departs

Porter had now been in Key West for five months, and events had gone very much in his favor. His ships had captured four brigs, sixteen schooners, and a sloop, and he boasted, "With my beggarly little force I have made the war with Spain my own." But the tide was beginning to turn against him. The Mexican government had failed to send the funds it had promised, and Porter was forced to use the proceeds from the sale of captured cargoes to pay his sailors and to buy provisions. When the president's order prohibiting the entry of prizes reached Key West, this source of income was cut off.

Fearful of the loss of commerce with Cuba because of Porter's depredations, newspaper editors demanded that Porter be forced to leave. The U.S. Navy was ordered to send a ship to Key West to verify that Porter was complying with the prohibitions against bringing in prizes and sending out commerce raiders. In August, Porter slipped through the blockade and sailed to New Orleans. At a gala banquet, he was toasted as a hero, but he had come for a more serious purpose. Lying at the mouth of the Mississippi was Mexico's newest and finest man-of-war, the twenty-two-gun brig *Guerrero*. She was full of ammunition and stores but short on experienced seamen. Porter circulated recruiting handbills in the city promising good pay and prize money, and soon he had seventy volunteers ready to enlist in the Mexican Navy. The U.S. District Attorney, apparently not one of Porter's hero worshippers, immediately recognized the recruiting operation as a violation of neutrality and arrested the men as they were sailing downriver to join the *Guerrero*. However, another group of one hundred volunteers managed to pass down the river without being intercepted. Six months later, during the *Guerrero*'s losing fight with a Spanish frigate, those recruits had cause to regret not being stopped in the Mississippi.

In reply to continuing charges in newspapers, Porter denied that he was violating U.S. neutrality but offered to leave Key West as soon as he was officially ordered to do so and the Spanish blockade was withdrawn. At the end of August, before Porter could return to Key West, both conditions were met. The Spanish blockaders returned to Havana, and the Key West collector of customs ordered the Mexican ships to leave. When Porter read newspaper accounts of their departure, he quickly issued a press release. In his usual nobody-tells-me-what-to-do manner, he claimed that it was he, not the Key West collector, who had ordered the squadron to sail, and he had done so in order to avoid further embarrassment to the United States government.

The Mexican Squadron returned to Vera Cruz just as the Mexican economy collapsed and, with the exception of single-ship commerce raids, never put to sea again. In February of 1828, the *Guerrero*, under the command of Porter's nephew, Capt. David H. Porter, fought the greatly superior sixty-four-gun Spanish frigate *Lealtad* and was badly damaged and captured. Casualties were heavy on both sides. On the *Guerrero*, 80 men out of a crew of 186 were either killed or wounded. Captain Porter was among those killed, and Commodore Porter's son, fifteen-year-old Midshipman David Dixon Porter, was taken prisoner.

Following the loss of the *Guerrero*, Porter's fortunes continued to decline. The Mexican government was unable to furnish enough money to

Battle between Spanish frigate *Lealtad* and Mexican brig *Guerrero* in which Commodore Porter's nephew, Captain David H. Porter, was killed and his son, Midshipman David Dixon Porter, was taken prisoner (copied by Mariners' Museum from *Memoir of Commodore Porter of the U.S. Navy,* J. Munsell, 1875. From the collections of The Mariners' Museum, Newport News, Virginia)

pay his salary or that of his sailors, let alone to maintain the ships. Porter wrote, "I am entirely destitute of funds and were it not for the charity of my friends, should absolutely perish from want." Finally, in September of 1828, he resigned his commission and returned to the United States. President Andrew Jackson, a great admirer of Porter, appointed him consul-general to Algiers. Porter later became minister to Turkey.

During the course of two commands based at Key West, Commodore Porter's forces achieved considerable success at sea, but his naval triumphs were overshadowed by personal disaster. A court martial ended his antipiracy command and U.S. Navy career, and bankruptcy awaited him as he surrendered his Mexican command. Despite this, a year after he left the Mexican service, he wrote a glowing letter to the Secretary of the Navy boosting Key West as the ideal site for a naval base. His recommendation undoubtedly had much to do with the U.S. Navy's permanent return to Key West.

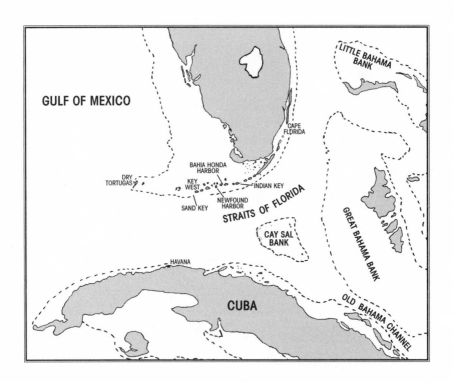

Chapter 6

REVENUE CUTTER MEN

Revenue Cutter Operations in the Straits and the Keys

A topsail schooner mounting six guns and flying a red-and-white vertically striped ensign rounded into the wind and dropped anchor in the harbor of Key West. Crewmen furled the sails and lowered a boat into the water. Four seamen in blue uniform jackets, white trousers, and broad-brimmed black hats manned the boat. In a few minutes, the captain, wearing a blue coat with gold epaulets, white pantaloons, and a cocked hat, climbed down into the boat. At his order, the seamen shoved off from the side of the vessel and began rowing toward the docks along the shore. The date was January 26, 1829, and the schooner was the U.S. Revenue Cutter *Marion*, seven days out of Savannah. Her captain had orders to report to the collector of customs to receive instructions for conducting another of the cutter's periodic law-enforcement patrols in the Keys.

Revenue cutters were no strangers to Keys waters. When the *Marion* dropped anchor in Key West, the Revenue Cutter Service (also called the U.S. Revenue Marine) had been in existence for thirty-two years. Forerunner of the U.S. Coast Guard, the service was formed by an act of Congress in 1790. Under the secretary of the treasury, its mission was to enforce the revenue laws for the collection of customs and tonnage duties which were then the principal source of income for the operation of the federal government. Between 1828 and 1832, revenues at the Key West custom house averaged about forty-five thousand dollars annually.

Revenue cutters first saw service in the Straits of Florida during the Quasi-War with France (1798–1801), when the cutters were transferred to operate under U.S. Navy orders. Two cutters, the *Governor Jay* and the *General Greene,* served with Commodore Stephen Decatur's squadron to protect American merchant vessels from the depredations of French privateers in the waters off the northern coast of Cuba. In March 1798, the eight-gun *General Greene* captured the French privateer twelve-gun schooner *Marsouin* in the straits north of Havana.

Two events in 1819 brought about regular revenue cutter patrols in Keys waters: One was the signing of the treaty transferring the territory of Florida to the United States; the other was the assignment of responsibility to the Revenue Cutter Service for suppressing the slave trade and piracy. In August of the same year, the cutters *Louisiana* and *Alabama,* while cruising north of the Dry Tortugas, chased a suspected pirate schooner. Upon being hailed to heave to, the schooner's crew discharged a volley of musket fire which wounded the first officer and two seamen on the *Louisiana.* A few minutes later, the *Alabama* fired a broadside which killed two of the pirates and drove the rest of them below decks. Boarding parties quickly secured the vessel and discovered that it was the *Bravo,* one of Jean Lafitte's pirate fleet.

The cutters' boat crews also boarded and captured a nearby schooner that proved to be a Spanish vessel the *Bravo* had captured. Passengers who had been on the Spanish schooner told the cutters' officers that the pirates had robbed them of all their possessions, including the clothes they were wearing. When the female passengers had begged the pirates to let them have something to cover themselves, the cutthroats had simply drawn their swords and cursed them.

Three years later, as the first settlers were arriving at Key West, the *Alabama* was patrolling the Keys again. This time she captured three sloops—two Bahamian and one American—that were transporting slaves. The cutters *Florida* and *Pulaski* were the next to patrol the Keys, and in 1824, the *Florida* captured a Spanish schooner, manned by a Colombian prize crew, that was attempting to smuggle sugar ashore on one of the Keys.

The Treasury Department ordered the *Florida* to patrol the Keys and the southwest coast of Florida again in 1827. Her sailing orders included a requirement to assist captains of wrecked ships in preserving their cargoes if requested to do so. If the wrecked ship was abandoned, the cutter was to take as much cargo as possible onboard and ship the rest aboard any available American vessel. Another unusual duty assigned to the *Florida* was to apprehend any persons or vessels engaged in cutting and carrying away valuable timber from the public lands in Florida.

The orders cautioned the captain of the *Florida* to load a six-month supply of provisions and other stores as he should not expect to be able to purchase any at Thompson's Island (Key West), or even at Pensacola or St. Augustine. If he ran low, he could sail to Mobile to replenish.

The *Florida's* authorized crew strength, exclusive of officers, was fifteen seamen, a cook, and a steward. If through injury, illness, death, or desertion the cutter needed replacements, the captain's orders again authorized him to sail to Mobile, or even New Orleans, to get them. Otherwise, except for stress of weather or necessary repairs, he was not to leave his cruising grounds.

The Cutter Marion on Patrol in the Keys

When the *Marion* dropped anchor in Key West harbor in January 1829, she was commanded by Capt. John Jackson. Jackson had taken command the previous May, and he came with a distinguished record. In his two previous commands, the *Dallas* and the *Louisiana,* he had captured seven pirate vessels, three slavers, and two privateers.

The *Marion,* built on the lines of a Baltimore clipper, was sixty-five feet long and displaced seventy-eight tons. With her large sail area and well-shaped hull she was able to outsail most vessels she met with. Four eighteen-pounder carronades and two four-pounder long guns backed up her authority to enforce U.S. revenue laws. In addition to the captain and two lieutenants, she was manned by a crew of twenty, including a boatswain, gunner, carpenter, sailmaker, cook, and steward.

The *Marion* was no newcomer to the Keys. In 1826, under Lieutenant

United States Revenue Cutter *Marion* patrolled the Keys to enforce revenue laws in the 1830s. (drawing by Henry Rusk in *The History of American Sailing Ships* by Howard I. Chapelle, courtesy of W. W. Norton & Company)

Doane, she conducted a six-month cruise in Florida waters. At Key West in December of that year, the captain of a ship which had just been refloated after going aground at Sand Key asked Doane to assist in quelling a mutiny among the slaves he was carrying from Alexandria, Virginia, to New Orleans (although importation of slaves into the U.S. had been outlawed in 1807, interstate transportation was still legal). An armed boat crew from the *Marion* boarded the ship and secured the ringleaders in irons.

The following year, with Doane still in command, the *Marion* was asked to provide assistance in an entirely different situation involving slaves. A Spanish slave ship had wrecked on the reef off Key Largo while being chased by a British warship. The Spanish crew seized an American wrecking schooner and an American fishing smack and forced them to carry 398 of the captive Africans to Cuba. A wrecking sloop, which had taken 121 slaves off the wreck, escaped seizure and carried them to Key West.

With rumors circulating that a Spanish brig was on the way from Cuba to recapture the Africans by force, they were placed in the custody of the deputy marshal. Some local residents made attempts to bribe or force the marshal to turn the slaves over to them. The marshal sent an urgent plea for help to the captain of the *Marion*. The captain sent an officer and several armed men to help the marshal protect the Africans. When it became apparent that the Africans would not be safe in Key West, they were taken to St. Augustine with the *Marion* serving as escort.

The *Marion*'s log from 1829 to 1832 has been preserved on microfilm at the National Archives. During those years, her home station was Charleston, but she conducted patrols in the Keys on an average of three times a year. The following narrative, derived from the *Marion*'s log from January through March 1829, in conjunction with other sources, provides a unique view of revenue cutter operations in the early years of Keys settlement.

When Jackson entered the Key West custom house on January 26, the collector of customs, William Pinckney, greeted him and inquired about his voyage. Jackson told him that he had lost one of the cutter's boats in a gale on the voyage north but had been able to replace it at Savannah. He said the *Marion* would be ready to begin operations as soon as the crew finished gathering stove wood and filling water tanks. Pinckney advised Jackson to be on the lookout for certain wreckers from Indian Key whom he suspected were smuggling cargoes they salvaged from wrecks by hiding them on remote Keys. When a favorable opportunity arose, he said, they would recover the goods and dispose of them without legal proceedings or duty fees.

Three days later, the *Marion* departed Key West, sailed eastward, and anchored that night off the Saddle Bunch Keys. In the morning, the captain dispatched the first lieutenant and five men in the barge (one of the cutter's two boats) to patrol the shallow waters of the Keys where the *Marion,* with a nine-and-a-half-foot draft, could not go.

The *Marion* continued eastward in Hawk Channel. Off Big Pine Key, the captain sent the second lieutenant in the other boat to board and inspect two wrecking vessels anchored in Newfound Harbor. That night, the cutter anchored in Bahia Honda Harbor. At 3:00 A.M., the barge returned, "having been to windward as far as Indian Key [a distance of nearly fifty miles]." Considering the total lack of navigational aids and the poor charts then available, the first lieutenant's feat in sailing from Indian Key to Bahia Honda in the middle of the night bears witness to the exceptional seamanship and navigational skills of the revenue cutter seamen.

After a stop at Key West, the *Marion* sailed westward to the Dry Tortugas. Sighting two fishing smacks, she took up chase. When they failed to heave to, Jackson ordered a musket fired. They continued to sail on, so he ordered the gun crew to fire a cannon, first with a blank charge and then twice "shotted" (with ammunition). Seeing the splash of cannonballs close aboard, the fishing captains luffed up and resigned themselves to a visit

Smuggler being chased by revenue cutter tacks into shallow water among Keys (from an illustration in *Smugglers and Smuggling*, A. Hyatt Verrill, New York: Duffield & Co., 1924)

from the cutter's boarding officer. The officer checked the ship's papers and cargo manifest and inspected the cargo holds. If he found any violations, they were not noted in the log. On that same day, the *Marion's* officers boarded seven more fishing and wrecking vessels in the Tortugas.

Working her way back to the east, the *Marion* cruised off the lower Keys for another week during which time her officers boarded and checked the cargo manifests of two large square-riggers bound for New Orleans. While the cutter was anchored in Bahia Honda Harbor one night, a heavy gale struck. The officer on watch called out all hands to send down the yards and topgallant masts, house the topmasts (to reduce windage aloft), and veer out more anchor line. The *Marion* rode out the gale and, after another brief visit to the Dry Tortugas, returned to Key West to replenish her water supply.

In March, after a quick sweep of the upper Keys, Jackson received orders from the collector to search along the north coast of Cuba for a pirate schooner that had taken four American merchant vessels and killed their crews. The *Marion* made two searches along the Cuban coast but was unable to find the pirate vessel. On March 26, she left Cape Florida to return to Savannah. In a two-month period she had been on patrol for thirty-eight days and in port at Key West for twenty-one. This was typical. On average, the *Marion* spent two-thirds of her time patrolling the Keys and one-third in port to reprovision and perform ship's maintenance.

Despite the reported prevalence of smuggling in the Keys, arrests were rare. Out of 117 boardings recorded in the log between 1829 and 1832, the *Marion's* boarding officer found only two vessels with unmanifested cargo. On a Spanish schooner bound to New Orleans from Havana he found six thousand "Spanish segars" not included in her manifest. Aboard a wrecking sloop in the Dry Tortugas he found a more serious violation. The sloop's captain told the boarding officer that he was bound for New London from Key West in ballast, that is, with no cargo. This aroused the officer's suspicions because the Dry Tortugas are not on the route between Key West and New London. Upon opening the cargo hatches, he saw a number of cotton bales. It was apparent that on some previous date, the sloop's captain had concealed the cotton, salvaged from a wreck, on one of the Tortugas islands. After clearing Key West in ballast, he had returned to the island and loaded the cotton. The boarding officer told the sloop's captain he must return to Key West and surrender to the collector of customs.

One of the *Marion*'s biggest problems while operating in the Keys was obtaining sufficient quantities of fresh water. Supplies at Key West often ran low, and on one occasion, the cutter had to sail to Havana to fill her tanks because there was no other water available. The cutter's crew subsisted principally on pickled or salted beef and pork, beans, and bread, but occasionally dined on fresh turtle or fish they caught. A daily ration of whiskey helped to break the monotony of the diet. Watch duties and ship's work continued seven days a week at sea. In port, ship's work went on every day except Sunday and Christmas Day. The captain granted one day's shore liberty for the crew on arrival in Charleston, Savannah, and Havana, but not in Key West. Revenue cutter seamen were paid fourteen dollars per month, while merchant seamen earned sixteen dollars per month. When two of the crew deserted in Havana, they probably did so to ship aboard a merchant ship.

Another concern while operating in the Keys was the possibility of an outbreak of malarial fever. In October of 1831, one of *Marion*'s crewmen died of fever at Key West. The following log entry illustrates the watch officer's matter-of-fact attitude toward his death:

"Oct. 28. At 10 A.M. Dr. Strobel visited our sick man. Advised to land him as soon as possible. Sent him ashore with four men to carry him.

Oct. 29. William Sharp expired. Cut a load of wood. Crew attended funeral of deceased."

Marion's Officers Lend a Hand in a Keys Election

It was not until 1831 that aid to vessels in distress became an official function of the Revenue Cutter Service. Even before that order was issued, the *Marion*'s log shows many incidents in which the *Marion* assisted other vessels. She furnished food and water to the starving crew of a brig, sent medicine to the sick captain and mate of a schooner, helped free a vessel that was aground, and arrested the leaders of a potential mutiny on an American merchant ship at Havana.

But there was another type of assistance rendered by the *Marion*'s crew which does not appear in her log. In May 1829, an election was held in Monroe County to elect a territorial delegate to Congress. The principal candidates were Colonel White and Colonel Gadsen, and in Monroe County, they were vying for the votes of just a few more than one hundred voters. For unknown reasons, it appears that Captain Jackson and his two lieutenants, Day and Harby, were more than a little anxious to help Colonel White win. On May 5, while anchored at Indian Key, the two lieutenants herded the crew ashore to the polling place and told them to cast their votes for Colonel White. Three of the men refused to vote for White and, as a consequence, had their whiskey rations stopped the next day.

One month later, the *Marion* was anchored at Key West when an election for representative to the territorial legislative council was being held. Once again, the officers led the crew ashore to the polling place. But this time the inspector of elections, Pardon Greene, refused to let them vote. He told them that their proper voting place was at their home port, Charleston. Jackson argued at length with Greene, to no avail. Not to be denied, the officers marched the crew back to the cutter and had them remove their uniforms. Dressed in ordinary seamen's working clothes, the men returned to the polling place and began voting. Most of them had cast their ballots before Inspector Greene saw through the deception and ordered them away.

The Key West newspaper, *The Register,* observed that without the votes of the twenty *Marion* crewmen at Indian Key, Colonel White would have lost in Monroe County. The editor questioned the legality of the votes, but in the next issue, he hastened to add that he had not meant to insinuate that Captain Jackson had exerted undue influence on the crew's votes. Four other citizens, angered by the *Marion's* interference in their elections, wrote letters to the secretary of the treasury describing what had taken place at the polls at Indian Key and Key West. One of them was Pardon Greene and another was Samuel Sanderson, captain of a wrecking schooner.

One might wonder why a wrecker (Sanderson) took any interest in the matter. The answer appears in the *Marion's* log. Three days before the election at Indian Key, one of the cutter's officers arrested Sanderson for a violation of revenue laws. On the day of the election he was confined on Indian Key. The next day, as he was about to be taken out to the cutter, he resisted and fought with his escort. While onboard the *Marion* as a prisoner, he observed that some of the crewmen's whiskey rations were stopped for their refusal to vote as directed. It was Sanderson who reported this incident in a letter to the secretary of the treasury.

The secretary of the treasury ordered the collector of customs at Key West to investigate charges that Captain Jackson had allowed the crew to go ashore to vote to the prejudice and neglect of the public service, had allowed the use of deceptive art to obtain their votes, had exerted an improper influence on controlling the votes of the crew, and had permitted his officers to do the same. Unfortunately, the report of the investigation has not been found. Presumably, Jackson got off with a warning or a reprimand, because he remained in command of the *Marion* until he was relieved by Lt. Robert Day in 1832 and commanded other cutters until he was lost at sea in 1840.

Audubon Rides the Marion

In April 1832 at Charleston, Lieutenant Day, now in command of the *Marion,* welcomed aboard the noted ornithologist John Audubon, accompanied by his dog Plato, taxidermist Henry Ward, and landscape painter George Lehman. Over the next six weeks, the *Marion* carried Audubon and his party on their search for new species of birds in the Florida Keys. The cutter made extended stops at Indian Key, Key West, and the Dry Tortugas to facilitate Audubon's work.

Audubon is mentioned only once in the *Marion's* log. At the Tortugas an entry reads, "Crew employed in gathering shells for Audubon Esq." In fact, the officers and crew did much more to help him. They rowed him to distant Keys, helped him shoot birds for specimens, and gave him much valuable information on the habits of Keys birds. Lieutenant Coste told him that young sooty terns "have been known to collect there [Dry Tortugas] for the purpose of breeding, since the oldest wreckers on that coast can recollect; and that they usually arrive in May, and remain until the beginning of August." From some of the seamen Audubon learned that laughing gulls eat the young terns after they are hatched. In his description of the tropic bird, he acknowledges that the specimens for his drawing were shot by "my kind friend Robert Day, Esq. of the United States Revenue Cutter, the *Marion.*"

One night while the *Marion* was at Indian Key, the residents held a dance. Captain Day and other members of his crew attended, but Audubon, ever the workaholic, chose to go on making drawings of specimens he had collected that day. The room in which he worked was next to the room in which the dance was held. He described the dance this way: "Two miserable fiddlers screwed their screeching silken strings—not an inch of catgut graced their instruments; and the bouncing of brave lads and fair lasses shook the premises to the foundation. One with a slip came down heavily on the floor, and the burst of laughter that followed echoed over the isle. Diluted claret was handed round to cool the ladies, while a beverage of more potent energies warmed their partners."

In his *Ornithological Biography,* Audubon several times refers to the *Marion* as the "Lady of the Green Mantle" but does not explain why. It may be that the cutter had a figurehead of a woman wearing a green cloak. It is evident that Audubon considered his work in the Keys a great success due in no small measure to the cooperation and efforts of, as he called them, the "gallant officers" and "brave tars" of the revenue cutter *Marion.*

Revenue Cutters in the Seminole War

During the Second Seminole War (1836–1842), revenue cutters operated in the Keys and along the southern mainland coast as an integral part of the naval forces engaged in the war against the Seminoles. The cutters transported troops and supplies, protected settlements and shipwrecked seamen from Indian attack, and formed part of the blockading forces to stop arms being smuggled to the Seminoles from Cuba and the Bahamas. Revenue marines in small boats searched inlets and rivers along the coast and participated in expeditions into the Everglades. Stories of revenue cutter exploits during the war are included in Chapter 7.

The Terrible Ordeal of the Cutter Morris

Hurricanes posed a serious threat to cutters operating in the Keys, with its few well-protected harbors, poor holding ground, and shoals and reefs in every direction. In 1844, an October hurricane blew the revenue cutter *Vigilant,* a fifty-six-foot sloop-rigged cutter with a crew of fourteen, out

United States Revenue Cutter *Morris,* lost at Key West in 1846 hurricane
(drawing by Henry Rusk in *The History of American Sailing Ships* by Howard I. Chapelle,
courtesy of W. W. Norton & Company)

of Key West harbor, and she capsized. Two seamen caught hold of a small canoe that floated free and, after two days and two nights clinging to it with the waves washing over them, were picked up by a passing vessel. They were the only survivors.

The Great Hurricane of 1846 was the most destructive storm to strike Key West in recorded history. Winds and waves swept away both the Sand Key and Key West lighthouses with a loss of twenty lives. At least five other citizens drowned as the water in the streets rose to five feet. Only eight of some six hundred houses survived undamaged, and all the waterfront wharves and warehouses were washed away or severely damaged. But the storm inflicted its most lethal impact on the vessels docked or anchored in the harbor. Not one of them escaped being sunk or driven aground. An officer of a brig wrote that more than forty seamen lost their lives.

Among the vessels anchored in the harbor on that fateful day was the U.S. Revenue Cutter *Morris*. Launched fifteen years earlier, the 112-ton *Morris* was 73 feet long, carried 6 six-pounder long guns, and was manned by a crew of 30. The *Morris*-class cutters were designed to achieve maximum speed. According to one writer, they could "eat right into the wind's eye." Because of the war with Mexico, the secretary of the treasury had ordered the *Morris* to Key West to protect American shipping in the Straits of Florida from Mexican privateers.

One of the *Morris'* officers, Lieutenant Pease, wrote an account of the cutter's terrifying ordeal during the storm. Here is his story, rewritten to clarify some of the lesser-known events and nautical terminology of those days.

Gale-force winds commenced about 10:00 A.M. on October 11, 1846, and reached hurricane force about 2:00 P.M. The *Morris* was riding to two anchors with 150 fathoms (900 feet) of chain out. Crewmen sent down the yards and secured them on deck to reduce windage aloft. The strain on the riding bitts (large posts to which anchor chains were secured) became so great that the crew rigged blocks and tackles to transfer some of the strain to other structural parts of the ship.

As the wind force increased, the cutter swung broadside to the direction of the wind and current, thereby greatly increasing the strain on the anchors (Pease estimated the current at twelve miles per hour). Fearful of parting the anchor chains, the captain ordered the mainmast cut away. The mast fell but failed to go over the side because the triatic stay (fore-and-aft line between masts) which connected it to the foremast had failed to part. The captain decided not to cut away the foremast because it could serve as a place of last refuge should the cutter sink at her anchors. With the mainmast swinging wildly overhead and threatening to break loose and plunge to the deck, a courageous seaman managed to climb the foremast. With a well-timed blow, he cut the stay, and the mainmast fell clear over the side.

By 4:00 P.M., the air was full of spray and rain, and the wind was so strong that it was impossible to face into it for more than a second. With waves beginning to wash completely over the deck, the captain ordered all hands to go below and batten down the hatches. Below decks, seamen worked frantically at the pumps and at bailing, trying to stem the rising water in the hull. The cutter labored heavily in the seas while roofs of houses, huge timbers, casks, and other wreckage from the town rushed by or dragged across the deck.

By 4:15 P.M., the water level in the hull had reached the height of the lowest ports and was continuing to rise. At this point, the starboard anchor chain parted, and the cutter began to drag her port anchor. Because the compasses were oscillating wildly and nothing could be seen through the raging storm, the crew had no idea in which direction they were being driven. They feared that they were headed for the reef where, once they struck, the hull would be torn open and they would sink.

The captain now ordered the foremast to be cut away. No sooner was this accomplished than a huge wave struck the ship, rolling it over on its side. The impact carried away bulwarks, one of the ship's boats, davits, and a small house on the quarterdeck. Every moveable object on deck was swept away. To right the vessel, the crew heaved the guns on the lee side overboard.

For the next hour, the cutter continued to drag anchor at the mercy of the wind and current, with the crew expecting her to sink at any moment. Instead, the *Morris* ran aground in shoal water and, simultaneously, the port anchor chain parted. Through the long night, the stoutly built hull pounded heavily on the bottom but did not break up.

The next morning as the storm abated, the cutter's crew saw that they had been driven some three miles to the northwest of the harbor across water that normally was only two or three feet deep (the *Morris* drew nine feet). All around they saw the remains of other vessels—a ship (a large, three-masted square rigger) rolled over on her side; three brigs and three schooners, all dismasted; three vessels sunk in the deeper water of a small channel; and four more bottom-up.

Later examination revealed that the *Morris* had stranded in water normally two feet deep and had bilged (her underwater hull was torn open). She was a total loss, but mercifully, all her crew had survived the terrible ordeal.

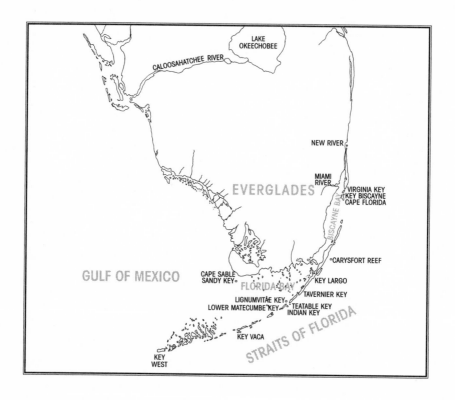

Chapter 7

NAVAL INDIAN HUNTERS

Seminole War Reaches the Keys

"*T*he Indians!!! Horrible Intelligence from the Seat of the War," screamed the headline of the *Key West Inquirer* of January 16, 1836. Below the headline, frightened citizens read news of Indian attacks which signaled the outbreak of the Second Seminole War— the longest, costliest, and bloodiest Indian war in U.S. history, and the only Indian war in which the U.S. Navy, along with units of the Revenue Cutter Service, played a substantial role.

Hostilities erupted in December 1835 as the deadline for removal of the Florida Indians to a reservation in the West neared. Determined to fight rather than be banished from their homeland, the Seminoles launched surprise attacks on military units and civilian plantations.

At the time the Seminoles went on the warpath, there were only four settlements in south Florida outside of Key West. On the mainland, a few pioneers had settled at New River (Fort Lauderdale today) and around the mouth of the Miami River. In the upper Keys, a less-than-scrupulous wrecking captain named Jacob Housman had established a prosperous wrecking settlement on tiny Indian Key. In the middle Keys, another small group of wreckers, fishermen, and farmers eked out an existence on the eastern end of Key Vaca.

The few Seminole bands in south Florida lived along both coasts and around Lake Okeechobee. The natives along the southeast coast were no strangers to the few white settlers around the Miami River and the New River. They visited the settlements to trade game and hides for liquor, clothing, guns, and ammunition. A few even worked on the settlers' farms.

The natives on the southwest coast had a long association with the Spaniards who came from Cuba to fish and to trade. These Spanish fishermen made it a point to establish friendly relations with the natives. After the United States acquired Florida and began measures to force the Seminoles to move to a western reservation, the Spanish fishermen urged them to resist removal and supplied them with arms. Among the natives of the southwest coast was a band of about one hundred Spanish-speaking natives known as the Spanish Indians. Led by a powerful, six-foot warrior named Chakaika, they were destined to play a prominent role in the war in south Florida and the Keys.

First news of the Seminole uprisings reached Commodore Alexander Dallas onboard the U.S. Frigate *Constellation* at Havana on January 12, 1836. A schooner dispatched by the citizens of Key West to buy arms and ammunition for their defense brought a letter addressed to Dallas from William Whitehead, the collector of customs. Whitehead's letter informed the commodore that on December 28, 1835, a large band of Seminoles had ambushed a column of 108 soldiers under the command of Maj. Francis Dade as they were marching from Tampa Bay to Fort King. Only three soldiers survived the attack. Just one week later, a war party had murdered the family of William Cooley, a settler at New River. All the settlers on the southern mainland and the outlying Keys (except Indian Key)—some two hundred in number—had fled to Key West. The refugees reported that a large war party was moving toward the settlements at the Miami River and that the lighthouse on Cape Florida at the southern tip of Key Biscayne had been abandoned. The residents of Key West, Whitehead reported, were highly alarmed for their safety and requested that the commodore send a warship for their protection at the earliest possible moment.

As soon as he finished reading the letter, Dallas issued orders for the *Constellation* and the sloop-of-war *St. Louis* to make preparations to get under way for Key West. Their departure at first light the next morning marked the first step in the U.S. Navy's participation in the war against the Seminoles. As the war continued and Army forces gradually drove the Seminoles southward into the vast, watery wilderness of the Everglades, naval forces became more and more involved in the conflict. Eventually, in one of the strangest chapters in U.S. Navy history, naval officers, often reporting to Army commanders, led sailors and marines—and sometimes even soldiers—in land expeditions against the Seminoles. Two naval officers, Lt. Levi Powell and Lt. John McLaughlin, and one revenue marine officer, Lt. Napoleon Coste, pioneered the use of naval personnel in offensive operations against the natives in south Florida. The Florida Keys figured importantly in their operations: first, as the scene of search-and-blockade missions, and second, as bases for naval forces operating in the area.

When the *Constellation* and the *St. Louis* arrived at Key West, they found the residents had already taken steps to defend themselves. The leading citizens had formed a defense committee, called up the militia, and instituted nightly patrols on land and sea to provide early warning of the approach of any war parties.

The *Constellation* remained at Key West for almost a month. During that time, her sailors helped the citizens clear the woods at the edge of town to hamper the Seminoles' ability to launch a surprise attack. Dallas also dispatched a lieutenant and a detachment of sailors in a chartered schooner to carry a lighthouse keeper and four guards to Cape Florida to restore the light to operation. Several refugees from the Miami River settlement accompanied the expedition to try to find out what had happened to their homes. On arrival, the sailors constructed barricades for the lighthouse ground-floor doors and windows. The sight of an Indian campfire on the mainland convinced the settlers that it was not safe to return to their homes. Leaving the lighthouse keeper and his guards to face the natives alone, the detachment returned to Key West.

Needing crew replacements and provisions, the *Constellation* left Key West for Pensacola on February 9. The *Key West Inquirer* lamented, "We have no cannon, but must depend solely on muskets without bayonets, rifles, pistols, and a species of short broad swords or, more properly, cane-knives, for our defense." The inhabitants of Indian Key, only twenty-five miles from the mainland, had even greater cause for concern. Despite their fears, their leader, the notorious wrecking captain, Jacob Housman, was not about to abandon his forty-thousand-dollar empire to the savages. He formed a twenty-four-man militia comprising all the able-bodied white males and six Negro slaves. He advanced them pay and subsistence at regular Army rates, assuming he would ultimately be repaid by the government. Not surprisingly, the militiamen elected Housman their captain. With the help of all the settlers, the militia constructed defensive embankments and mounted six cannon at strategic points around the island.

Although there were no Seminole villages in the Keys, the islands were familiar territory to the natives of south Florida. They went there to fish and catch turtles, and they passed through the Keys on their voyages around the coast. After Indian Key was settled, the natives often went to the island in their dugouts to trade at the store. As a result, when the war began, they were well aware of the large stocks of clothing, provisions, knives, guns, and ammunition kept there.

Two months passed without incident while nightly patrols at Key West and lookouts at Indian Key remained on the alert. Then, in mid-March, an old Spaniard paddled up to Indian Key in a canoe. He told the islanders that he had come to trade at the store, but they did not believe him. The residents of Indian Key were well aware of the friendly relations that existed between most of the south Florida natives and the Spanish fishermen from Cuba, and they believed that the Spanish were supplying the Seminoles with arms and ammunition to resist removal.

The Indian Key militiamen grilled the Spaniard at length until he finally broke down and admitted that he had been accompanied by two natives who were waiting for him on a nearby key. A party of armed men manned a boat and began combing the neighboring keys. After a lengthy search, they captured the two natives on Lignumvitae Key. The militiamen placed the natives and the Spaniard under guard and interrogated them further. The natives boasted that there was a large war party encamped at Cape Sable that planned to attack Indian Key, Key Vaca (then deserted), and even Key West. With this intelligence, the islanders penned an urgent dispatch to Commodore Dallas at Pensacola to send a warship for their protection.

Because the Navy had no ships to spare, three revenue cutters—the *Washington,* the *Dexter,* and the *Jefferson*—had been transferred to Navy com-

Revenue cutters were transferred to Navy control to augment naval forces operating against the Seminoles in Florida (U.S. Coast Guard Collection, U.S. Coast Guard Academy)

mand in January to augment the naval forces available in Florida. Dallas ordered the *Dexter* to sail for Indian Key. In the meantime, the islanders saw more and more signs of the presence of warriors in the upper Keys.

It was May before the *Dexter* arrived. Despite the presence of the cutter, the natives continued to frequent the neighborhood, awaiting a favorable opportunity to attack. Soon after the *Dexter*'s arrival, the islanders transferred the two natives and the Spaniard to the cutter for safekeeping. Then, incredibly, on June 15, both natives managed to free themselves from their irons and jump overboard. One was shot and killed, but the other swam safely to an island about two miles distant. Shocked by the loss of his companions, the Spaniard, who was in poor health, died the next morning.

Just one month after her arrival, the *Dexter* was forced to sail to Pensacola for supplies. On the eve of her departure, the three leading citizens of Indian Key addressed to Commodore Dallas a strong appeal for the ship's quick return. They said they were convinced that the Indians were preparing to attack the island and would be much aided by the information the recently escaped spy brought them. As evidence of their belief, they reported, "We have long frequently witnessed their [the Seminoles'] fires between us and the Main Land and a few days Since, 4 Canoes was [*sic*] seen within a few miles of this Island. Several more were also Seen in the Bay [Florida Bay] between this and Cape Florida at one Sight and a large number almost every day for several days in succession."

The *Dexter* did not return to Indian Key until July, and in the meantime, the Seminoles picked a less well-defended outpost for their next raid—the lighthouse at Cape Florida. On the day of their attack, July 23, 1836, only two men manned the lighthouse: John Thompson, the keeper, and an elderly Negro assistant named Aaron Carter. The two keepers managed to get inside the tower before the attackers reached them. The warriors then set fire to the door, and soon the interior structure caught fire. The heat and flames forced the keeper and his assistant to retreat to the top of the tower, where they lay down on a narrow circular platform around the outside of the light. When the fire reached the lantern room, it broke the glass and set Thompson's clothes on fire. Thompson decided to end his suffering by throwing a keg of gunpowder down into the inferno. But instead of killing him, the explosion blew out the fire.

The two men lay on the platform through the night as the Seminoles continued to fire at them. Carter soon died of his wounds, but despite being hit with six rifle balls, Thompson survived. In the morning, assuming both men were dead, the warriors plundered the keeper's quarters and departed. Situated some seventy feet off the ground with no means to get down and unable to walk even if he did, the wounded Thompson lay suffering in the burning sun all day long.

Fortunately for Thompson, the schooner *Motto*, manned by a U.S. Navy crew under Lt. Thomas Leib, USN, was heading south along the coast, returning from the investigation of a wreck. The schooner was about twelve miles away when her crew heard the explosion of the gunpowder keg and proceeded toward the lighthouse to investigate.

Delayed by contrary winds and currents, the *Motto* did not reach Cape Florida until late in the afternoon. Despite repeated attempts, it was not until the next morning that the sailors were able to get Thompson down from the tower. After treatment at Key West, he was sent to Charleston, South Carolina, where, although crippled, he eventually recovered.

After the attack on the Cape Florida lighthouse, there were no further signs of Seminoles in the Keys. The arrival of the revenue cutter *Washington*, assigned to patrol the southern coast and the Keys to stop arms smuggling to the natives, helped to restore a degree of calm. The Key West volunteer patrolmen discontinued their nightly rounds, and a few settlers began returning to their homes on Key Vaca.

With the southern mainland in complete possession of the Seminoles, the closest white-man's outpost to hostile territory was the lightship at Carysfort Reef. To vary their dull routine and diet, the crew had planted a farm-garden on Key Largo. On October 5, 1836, a band of about seventy natives crossed Florida Bay to Key Largo and destroyed the garden and storage buildings. Three days later, they attacked a small schooner riding at anchor at Tavernier Key. The crew of five hastily abandoned ship and, although two were wounded, escaped in their small boats. The Seminoles looted the vessel and then burned her.

Lt. Levin Powell, USN—First to Lead Naval Forces Ashore

Once again, the inhabitants of Indian Key saw the glow of campfires on neighboring keys and made preparations to defend themselves. But just a few days later, the arrival of an expedition of fifty sailors and ninety-five marines onboard the revenue cutter *Washington* calmed their fears. Under the command of Lt. Levin Powell, USN, the force was on its way to attack a party of some two hundred Seminoles believed to be at Cape Florida or New River.

Powell was no newcomer to naval shore expeditions against the Seminoles. Earlier that year, in March and April, he had led small boat expeditions of sailors and revenue marines scouting the coast and rivers in the Tampa Bay and Charlotte Harbor areas. In one expedition, Powell joined his forces with a detachment of soldiers and scouted on land along the banks of a river. The colonel in command of the soldiers said of Powell's men, "when they left their boats they [the sailors and revenue marines] rivalled the best soldiers."

On arrival at Indian Key, Powell hired William Cooley, the former settler at New River whose family had been killed by the Seminoles, to serve as a guide. Also accompanying the expedition as a guide was Stephen R. Mallory, on a leave of absence from his job as inspector of customs at Key West. Mallory, who later became a U.S. senator from Florida and, still later, secretary of the Confederate Navy, accompanied the expedition in his own schooner-rigged whaleboat with a crew of Navy seamen. He was well acquainted with the southeastern Florida coast, having spent a year helping to develop a plantation at the mouth of the Miami River. He became friendly with the natives, learned their language, and even accompanied them on hunting trips.

Seeing smoke from campfires on Key Largo, Powell decided to set a trap to catch the warriors as they returned to the mainland. The expedition had four boats small enough to negotiate shallow Florida Bay. Powell obtained two more from Indian Key, one of them provided by Jacob Housman. Housman was only too happy to help the expedition. At the time, he was trying to get Indian Key designated a port of entry so he could bring wrecked ships and cargoes to his domain instead of to his rivals in Key West. In his typical scheming fashion, he offered each sailor and marine a glass of grog in return for a signature on his port-of-entry petition. Nearly all signed happily, some more than once.

Powell divided his forces into two groups. One group was to circle around the northern end of Key Largo. The other, with Powell in charge, was to move into Florida Bay under cover of darkness, hoping to catch the Seminoles on the water returning to the mainland. When, by the next afternoon, none had appeared, Powell began scouting along the shore. He sighted two warriors in a dugout and chased them. When the distance between the boats and the dugout had closed sufficiently, Powell ordered his men to fire, but their shots missed. The warriors beached their dugout and ran into the woods. Powell's men landed and followed their trail to a hastily aban-

Lt. Powell, USN, was first to lead sailors, marines, and soldiers on scouting expeditions into the Everglades (courtesy of U.S. Naval Historical Center)

doned campsite. Although all the Seminoles escaped, they had been forced to leave their dugouts, fishing gear, and provisions; these Powell destroyed.

During the next two months, Powell's expedition explored the east coast as far north as Indian River and the west coast as far as Charlotte Harbor, and made the first penetration of the Everglades by white men. They found no natives but learned many valuable lessons for future operations against the Seminoles in the Everglades, particularly the need for lightweight, shallow-draft boats. Commodore Dallas wrote the secretary of the Navy that Powell's men were "due much credit for their perseverance and exertions under circumstances of privation for such a length of time in open boats."

At the end of the first year of the war, the Seminoles still held undisputed possession of the southern mainland and continued to menace the small community on Indian Key. Seven months elapsed before the Seminoles appeared in the Keys again. On the morning of June 23, 1837, a band of natives ambushed and killed the captain of the Carysfort Reef lightship and one of his crewmen as they stepped ashore on Key Largo to gather wood for the ship's stove.

The inhabitants of Indian Key, greatly alarmed by the news of the ambush and the sight of smoke from campfires on nearby keys, addressed an urgent appeal to the secretary of the treasury to send a revenue cutter for their protection. In an uncanny prediction of the fate that awaited them three years hence, the islanders wrote:

> The peculiar Situation of Indian Key renders it liable to incursion from these hostile savages more than any other location on the coast; the temptation too is considerable inasmuch as a large store is kept on the key which is at all times filled with provissions [*sic*] and munitions of war for the use of the inhabitants and wreckers engaged on the coast, and these facts are well known to the Indians, they having previous to the breaking out of hostilities been in the habit of trading at this store.
>
> Your petitioners would further shew [*sic*] that it has already cost the inhabitants of the Island and those interested therein upwards of $9,000 in protecting their families & property which expense falls heavily upon them and ought not to be borne by them. Unless some assistance is rendered them by the government to whom they pay burthensome [*sic*] taxes for protection, they fear all their personal efforts will prove unavailing.

The secretary of the treasury ordered the cutter *Jefferson* to proceed to Indian Key, but other events intervened and she was sent elsewhere. In the meantime, the Seminoles had disappeared from the Keys, and the settlers on Indian Key breathed a sigh of relief.

In a letter to the secretary of war written in September 1837, Powell offered to conduct another campaign in the Everglades with a combined force of sailors, marines, and soldiers using small boats that could negotiate the shallow water. From December until the following April, Powell led a series of scouting expeditions up rivers and into the Everglades. In January, at the Jupiter River, he encountered a well-concealed band of Seminoles. When the officer leading one group of sailors was wounded and put out of action, some of the sailors began a panicked retreat. Powell rallied the remainder and, although wounded himself, prevented a rout. Before the engagement was over, the Seminoles had killed four of his men and wounded twenty-two.

In February, Powell constructed a supply depot on Key Biscayne and used it as a base of operations until he left the area. Gen. Thomas Jesup, the overall commander in Florida, commended Powell for his cooperation with the army and the value he brought to the campaign, but for unknown reasons, Powell never returned to the Florida war.

Lt. Napoleon Coste, USRM—Establishes First Base in the Keys

The revenue cutters *Campbell* and *Madison* were placed under Navy control in 1838 and ordered to patrol the southern coastline and the Keys. Their mission was to prevent arms smuggling and to protect shipping and settlers in the Keys. First Lt. Napoleon L. Coste, USRM, commanded the *Campbell*. He had been a Key West pilot before joining the U.S. Revenue Service in 1830 and had served aboard the cutter *Marion* when she operated in the Keys in the early 1830s. The *Campbell* was Coste's first command, and he was determined to make a success of it.

On arriving in Key West on February 1, 1838, Coste engaged Francis Watlington (then owner of what is today known as Key West's "Oldest House") as pilot. The cutter then sailed for Biscayne Bay to augment the naval forces there under Lieutenant Powell. Coste worked closely with Powell, and on occasion, revenue marine and Navy personnel manned scouting parties jointly.

In the course of five reconnoitering expeditions during February, the *Campbell's* men got their first taste of the hardships and frustrations of chasing Seminoles along the south Florida coast. They sailed and rowed in open boats along the shoreline for days at a time. They searched the densely forested rivers and creeks, were constantly on guard for an ambush, slept in the cramped confines of their craft, and were continually under attack from hordes of mosquitoes. Their very first mission was typical of other missions that followed. On their way to investigate fires seen at the north end of Key Biscayne, their boat ran aground. They waded ashore and fought their way through several miles of dense underbrush only to find their elusive foe had vanished.

At the end of February, the *Campbell* was diverted to other duties, including carrying Army dispatches, transporting troops and supplies, and convoying a steamer carrying Seminole prisoners. Coste also took time out to make repairs to the *Campbell's* deteriorating hull at Key West and Charleston and did not return to patrolling the Keys until August. In the meantime, with Powell's forces gone, the Seminoles burned the supply depot on Key Biscayne.

While anchored at Indian Key on September 15, Coste learned that a severe gale a week earlier had driven several vessels ashore north of Cape Florida, and a number of their crewmen had been killed by the Seminoles. He immediately got under way and headed north. In Biscayne Bay, he met Lt. John McLaughlin, USN, in the U.S. Schooner *Wave,* newly arrived in the area to command the close-in blockading forces. After a conference onboard the *Wave,* the two officers formed a task group consisting of thirty seamen and marines from the *Wave* and twenty-four seamen from the *Campbell* under the overall command of McLaughlin. Lt. John Faunce, USRM, the *Campbell's* second lieutenant, led the revenue marines.

At midnight, the expedition got under way in four boats and headed north. At daylight, they sighted a brig ashore about eight or nine miles distant. At noon, Faunce found three canoes onshore and sighted natives on the brig. Faunce and ten of his men landed and worked their way through a swamp, while McLaughlin's group continued to approach in the boats. When in position, Faunce ordered his men to charge, hoping to trap the natives between his force and the advancing boats. The warriors, about eighteen in number, fled into the swamp. Faunce's men killed three of them but, totally exhausted from the long row and slog through the swamp, were unable to follow.

Encouraged by this success, Coste determined to adopt an even more aggressive strategy. To make best use of his forces, he needed a shore base to stock supplies and maintain his boats. He picked Tea Table Key because it was close to the wrecker's settlement on Indian Key which had a store, large water cisterns, and frequent communication with Key West and the mainland. The *Campbell's* men spent most of the month of October clearing Tea Table and building a boat house and a storehouse of thatched palmettos. Coste named his outpost Fort Paulding after the secretary of the Navy, James K. Paulding. The secretary might not have been so impressed with the honor bestowed on him had he seen the two miserable structures Coste called a fort.

Lt. Napoleon Coste established a base on Tea Table Key in 1838 to facilitate operations against Seminoles (watercolor by Naya Rydzewski)

Leaving some men behind to work on the buildings, the *Campbell* returned to Biscayne Bay with two barges in tow. On the evening of October 22, a lookout sighted fires in the vicinity of Bear Cut at the northern end of Key Biscayne. Coste sent a boat with muffled oars (wrapped in canvas to reduce noise from rubbing in rowlocks) to investigate, and the crew returned to report sighting a party of warriors. Coste and twenty-five revenue marines manned the two barges and headed up the bay. They sighted a party of natives encamped on Virginia Key, but as they were moving ashore, the warriors saw them and fired. The revenue marines returned the fire and killed three natives, but the rest escaped into the woods. In their haste, the Seminoles abandoned much valuable equipment, including two canoes, some rifles, rifle balls, and gunpowder. Attached to the powder pouches, Coste found seven scalps, presumably taken from the castaway seamen killed by the Seminoles after the September storm.

For the next six months, the *Campbell* and her boats stayed constantly on the move, searching the shorelines of the upper Keys, Florida Bay, and Biscayne Bay. Occasionally they discovered fresh trails or recent campsites but never again came face to face with their foe. Coste drove his ship and his crew to the limit of their endurance. In April 1839, while anchored at Key West, two seamen jumped overboard, swam ashore, stole a boat, and made good their escape. Another seaman, stationed on Tea Table Key, went over to Upper Matecumbe Key to hunt and was never seen again.

Wear and tear was also having its effect on the cutter. In any kind of a seaway she leaked so badly that the pumps had to be kept going constantly. With his ship literally sinking under him, Coste continued to pursue his mission. In March, he advised the secretary of the treasury that extensive sections of planking were rotten and that he did not consider his vessel seaworthy. Finally, in May, Coste and the *Campbell* were ordered North, never to return.

Lt. John McLaughlin, USN–Mosquito Fleet Leader

Young and ambitious, Lt. John T. McLaughlin, USN, was determined to get into the action when the Second Seminole War broke out. Seeing no opportunity for advancement at sea, he requested and was granted permission to serve with the Army in Florida. In the summer of 1837, he was seriously wounded during an engagement with the Seminoles and was disabled for six months. Undaunted by this experience, he returned to duty with the Army and was given command of a dozen flat-bottom troop transports. Inclined to be vainglorious, McLaughlin, despite the lowly nature of his little flotilla, assumed the title of "Commodore."

The secretary of war was concerned that the Navy's offshore blockade was not stopping the smuggling of arms to the Seminoles from Cuba and the Bahamas. He asked McLaughlin to submit suggestions for tightening the blockade. McLaughlin proposed the use of fast, shallow-draft schooners and gun barges to patrol the coast close in and to facilitate communications with Army outposts. Based on his recommendations, the Army authorized the purchase of the schooner-yacht *Wave* and two gun barges and asked the Navy to put McLaughlin in command.

The *Wave,* carrying the two gun barges onboard, arrived in the Keys just in time to proceed to the aid of the ships cast up on the shore north of Cape Florida during the September, 1838, gale. As previously related,

McLaughlin met Coste in the *Campbell* and participated in the attack against a band of Seminoles at the site of a wrecked brig. After this incident, McLaughlin assigned his forces to regular patrol areas and established a supply depot on Indian Key. The thirty-foot, single-masted gun barges—each manned by a crew of fifteen and mounting a swivel gun—patrolled among the upper Keys. The *Wave* and a chartered sloop, later exchanged for a schooner, patrolled along the reef and the southern coastline.

During the next seven months, McLaughlin's units explored every bay and inlet along the coast, charted the coastline, and aided ships in distress but had only fleeting contacts with the enemy. One of the barges sank while attempting to rescue the crew of a shipwrecked vessel. Chafing under the lack of action, McLaughlin began to formulate plans for a more aggressive role for his forces. But in May 1839, Gen. Alexander Macomb concluded a truce with the Seminoles, and in June, McLaughlin was forced to take the *Wave* north for crew replacements. He left the chartered schooner and the barge behind to continue the patrols.

In Washington, McLaughlin presented his ideas for a more aggressive strategy to the secretary of the Navy. He proposed to penetrate the Everglades in canoes and flat-bottom boats, capture the Seminole women and children, and destroy their settlements and crops. Impressed by the lieutenant's experience, innovative proposals, and action-oriented approach, the secretary gave him command of the newly-constructed, 150-ton schooner *Flirt* and authorized him to purchase the necessary flat-bottom boats and canoes.

McLaughlin did not get back to the Keys until January 1840. During his absence, Cdr. Isaac Mayo, USN, commanding the sidewheel steamer *Poinsett,* had been in charge of the blockade forces. With four additional barges, Mayo continued the patrols in the Keys and along the southern coast. The barges scouted up rivers but were too large to penetrate the Everglades proper. In July, a band of Seminoles attacked an Army trading post on the Caloosahatchee River, killing eighteen soldiers, and the truce came to an end.

In August, Mayo visited Indian Key and reported, "[I] Consider the post of great importance, for should the Indians capture it, they would be abundantly supplied with ammunition and arms, also a large supply of pro-

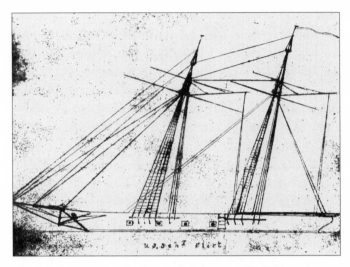

Lt. McLaughlin's flagship, U.S. Schooner *Flirt* (150 tons),
from a sketch in Flirt's logbook (copied from a print in "Journal
of a Cruise in the U.S. Brig *Truxton*," official U.S. Navy photograph)

visions." Accordingly, he stationed a gun barge with thirteen men under the command of a passed midshipman to defend the island.

Mayo returned to Indian Key in late September to find that malaria had broken out among the barge crew and that their camp was filthy. Two of the sick men died shortly after being carried aboard the *Poinsett,* and the passed midshipman died a few days later. In the meantime, a detachment of men sent ashore to clean up the camp also came down with the fever. Afraid the sickness would spread to the *Poinsett's* crew, Mayo sent the surgeon and his assistant, together with several nursing attendants, ashore to set up a hospital. Sailors erected a large tent made from sails. In a short while, the medical staff became ill, and one of the nursing attendants died. It was the first Navy hospital on Indian Key but not the last, and it was not the last time naval personnel would die there.

In November, Mayo wrote the secretary of the Navy that the suspected arms smuggling to the Seminoles did not exist and added that the wreckers cruising along the coast were an important factor in preventing it. His flagship plagued with mechanical problems, Mayo took the *Poinsett* north in December, and McLaughlin, arriving one month later, became the overall commander.

In addition to the *Flirt,* McLaughlin's forces included the schooner-yacht *Wave,* the chartered schooner *Otsego,* five gun barges, and about sixty flat-bottom boats and canoes ranging in length from ten to forty feet. The officers and men of McLaughlin's command called themselves the "Mosquito Fleet," the same name Porter's men had adopted for their antipiracy squadron. McLaughlin took over the shore base on Tea Table Key established by Lieutenant Coste and continued to use Indian Key as a supply depot. On Tea Table, sailors and marines underwent intensive training in handling the small boats and canoes and in firing small arms. They also set up a hospital for possible future casualties and for men who might come down with malaria.

The *Wave,* now under the command of Lt. John Rodgers, remained at Tea Table for almost two months while her carpenters and sailmakers constructed a new mainmast to replace the one lost on the voyage south. Entries in her log during this period provide a few glimpses of life aboard one of the Mosquito Fleet vessels. Based on the records of provisions received, the crew's standard fare was beef, pork, bread, and cheese with a daily ration of whiskey. On rare occasions, the monotony of the menu was relieved by the receipt of fresh turtle meat. Every few days, one-third of the crew went ashore to practice firing small arms. On February 15, sixteen volunteers under the command of Passed Midshipman Carter, together with another midshipman and a doctor, left the schooner on a one-week expedition to Cape Sable in company with a detachment from the *Otsego.*

Rodgers was a stern disciplinarian. Two days after arrival at Tea Table, despite a Navy regulation limiting commanding officers' punishments to no more than twelve lashes, Rodgers ordered a seaman to be flogged with twelve lashes for drunkenness, twelve more for insolence, and twelve more for quarreling. During the two months' stay at Tea Table, six more seamen suffered floggings of up to twenty-four lashes each for drunkenness or for riotous conduct ashore, and a petty officer was reduced in rate for drunkenness. One disgruntled seaman deserted while the *Wave* was taking on supplies at Key West—a poor choice for a place to escape. Three weeks later he was back aboard, lashed to the gratings, with all hands mustered to witness punishment. The log entry simply read that he was "punished with the cats for desertion." The number of strokes was not recorded, but undoubtedly, it was many times over that applied for drunkenness or riotous conduct.

Over the next six months, McLaughlin led his men on probes up rivers and streams along the southern coast and into the fringes of the Everglades. No Seminoles were found, but the sailors and marines learned how to paddle and pole their boats through the dense sawgrass and muck and how to live, eat, and sleep onboard their tiny craft for days on end.

In April, McLaughlin decided his men were ready for their first deep penetration into the Everglades. He hoped to surprise the natives by entering from the west instead of the east. He ordered the three schooners to rendezvous at Cape Sable before proceeding to Lostman Key to launch the expedition. The *Otsego* arrived at the cape first and sent twenty-four sailors and marines ashore to reconnoiter. No sooner were they ashore than they came under fire from a large war party estimated at fifty to eighty warriors. Only the arrival of reinforcements from the *Flirt* and the *Wave* about two hours later saved them from annihilation. Remarkably, no one was killed, but before the expedition could leave for Lostman Key, fever broke out and the attempt had to be abandoned.

Seminoles were not McLaughlin's only problem. A number of the *Flirt's* crew were black. While onshore at Key West on ship's business, the sheriff arrested several black sailors for violating a Florida law against the immigration of free blacks into the territory. With help from the judge of the superior court, McLaughlin obtained their release, but not before the sailors were forced to pay court costs. McLaughlin sought guidance from the Navy department for such occurrences in the future but received nothing but bureaucratic gobbledygook in reply.

In July, a Negro named John presented himself at Fort Dallas on the Miami River claiming to have escaped from the Seminoles after four years in captivity. He also volunteered the information that the Spanish Indians under Chief Chakaika were planning to attack Indian Key. The officers gave no credence to this intelligence. They considered ridiculous the idea that the natives would travel across thirty miles of water to attack a settlement under the guns of the Mosquito Fleet. The Army commander, afraid John might be a spy, slapped him in irons.

McLaughlin went to Fort Dallas to try to obtain John's services as a guide but was refused. He was allowed to talk to the prisoner, who was cooperative and even volunteered directions to Chakaika's island deep in the Everglades. Armed with this information, McLaughlin led an expedition to try to find Chakaika's hideout. But after just seven days of wandering in the sawgrass wilderness, his men were exhausted and he realized it was hopeless without a guide.

Despite this discouraging experience, McLaughlin was not about to give up. He made plans for another expedition with an even more ambitious goal: to cross the Everglades from coast to coast. Still hoping to get the services of John as a guide, he dispatched an urgent request to the war department for his release. He ordered his second-in-command, Lt. John Rodgers in the *Wave,* to proceed to the west coast with eighteen canoes and to wait for him to arrive with the Negro guide. On the way to his station, Rodgers stopped at Tea Table Key and took aboard all the able-bodied men, except Midshipman Murray and five sailors who remained there to care for the sick. The stage was now set for the most dramatic event of the Second Seminole War in the Keys.

Unbeknownst to Rodgers, a band of more than one hundred Spanish Indians under Chief Chakaika lay concealed on Lower Matecumbe Key. When they saw the *Wave,* crowded with men and canoes, sail away, they knew the moment had arrived to launch their attack. At 2:00 the next morning, August 7, 1840, the warriors beached seventeen dugout canoes on Indian Key and crept silently among the houses. Only the chance sleeplessness of a carpenter saved the inhabitants from annihilation. Looking out his door, he saw the canoes pulled up on the beach and awoke his neighbor. Together they headed toward Housman's house to spread the alarm. On the way, they accidentally stumbled across the warriors lying in wait to make their attack. Shots were fired, which awoke the settlers. In the darkness and confusion, most of the inhabitants found hiding places or escaped in boats, but the attackers discovered and killed five of them.

Those who escaped in boats reached a schooner anchored by Tea Table Key and informed Midshipman Murray of the attack. At dawn, Murray made preparations to counterattack. With the five able-bodied seamen left behind by Rodgers and seven or eight volunteers from among the sick, he manned two barges. The sailors lashed two four-pounder carriage guns to the thwarts and rowed toward Indian Key, about a mile away. Murray planned to cut off the warriors' retreat by destroying their canoes. As the barges neared the island, Chakaika's warriors, some concealed in the houses and others in a large group on the beach, began yelling and firing. A musket ball hit one of Murray's seamen in the thigh, wounding him severely. Several warriors succeeded in loading the island's six-pounder defense guns and fired them with good aim.

Murray's men returned the fire with their muskets and cannon, but on the third discharge, the hastily lashed four-pounders recoiled overboard. Greatly outnumbered and deprived of any means of destroying the canoes, Murray decided to retreat to Tea Table and prepare to defend the hospital and supply depot against attack. Instead of attacking Tea Table, however, the Indians devoted their efforts to looting the store and houses on Indian Key. In the afternoon, they set fire to the buildings and departed, carrying off a slave woman and three Negro children. One more victim of the attack, a boy, died in a cistern after the warehouse above it was set on fire.

With his little empire a smoldering ruin, Jacob Housman agreed to turn the island over to the Navy. McLaughlin was particularly anxious to have the use of the large water cisterns Housman had built. Over the next several months, McLaughlin transformed the devastated village into a bustling naval base. At a cost of about ten thousand dollars, carpenters constructed twelve new buildings, including barracks for two companies of marines, a hospital, storehouses, workshops, boat sheds, and sick officers' quarters (which also served as an office and storeroom). The hospital, despite its description by a Navy doctor as "literally nothing of a hospital," soon became the busiest place on the island.

Evidence that the Indians had not completely deserted the Keys came in October, three months after the raid on Indian Key. The captain of the U.S. schooner *Wave,* then lying at Indian Key, received an urgent plea from Charles Howe, Indian Key's postmaster and inspector of customs, to conduct a search for his overdue turtling schooner, the *Charles and Edward.* During the Indian Key raid, the Indians had attempted to destroy the schooner by setting it on fire, but it did not burn. When the schooner's two-man crew had finished repairing her, they asked Howe to let them go on a turtle-hunting trip. Incredibly, despite all that had happened, Howe gave his assent. After several days, they returned with a large load of turtles and reported they had seen no Indians. On October 6, they sailed again, but when they had not returned after eighteen days, Howe became concerned and went to the *Wave*'s captain for help.

After two days of combing Florida Bay and its connecting passages, boats from the *Wave* found the schooner partially sunk among the mangroves. There was no sign of her crew. The Indians had stripped her of all her gear, knocked holes in her hull, and set her on fire. But once again, the *Charles and Edward* refused to burn. In the cargo hold, the sailors found fifty turtles. In their destructive frenzy, the Indians had cut the heads off half of them. It was assumed that the Indians had killed the two crewmen at the time of the attack. Not until a year later was it learned, from a captured Indian, that the crewmen had been taken prisoner and held in captivity for several months. They had attempted to escape but were recaptured and tortured until they died.

About two weeks after the *Charles and Edward* was found, two turtling boats from Key Vaca foolishly ventured into Florida Bay. When they were near Sandy Key, just south of Cape Sable, a band of Indians in dugouts and boats began chasing them. The turtlers managed to escape and reported that they recognized the boats as those the Indians had stolen from Indian Key during the raid.

Chakaika's band had little time left to enjoy the spoils of their attack on Indian Key. Col. William Harney, USA, survivor of Chakaika's attack on the Army outpost on the Caloosahatchee River in July, 1839, was thirsting for revenge. In early December, using canoes borrowed from the Mosquito Fleet, he led an expedition of ninety soldiers into the Everglades. John, the slave who had escaped from the Indians, guided Harney's men to a hammock where Chakaika was hiding. Their attack caught the Indians completely unawares. The soldiers killed four warriors, including Chakaika, and Harney hanged five more who had been captured. Chakaika's sister was among the captured women. She told her captors that three Spaniards had come into the Everglades and supplied the Indians with salt and ammunition. One of them, named Domingo, she said, had advised Chakaika to attack Indian Key and assured him he would be successful.

Over the next two years, McLaughlin's forces, sometimes in company with Army contingents, conducted numerous expeditions into the depths of the Everglades, destroying the natives' camps, crops, and fields but seldom finding any Seminoles. In January 1841, an expedition led by McLaughlin became the first group of white men to cross the Everglades from coast to coast.

No campaign in the Second Seminole War was more demanding of human endurance than the one undertaken by the sailors and marines of the Mosquito Fleet. Under the burning sun, they poled and dragged their canoes across the trackless wilderness of the Everglades in search of an ever-elusive foe. The razor-sharp sawgrass cut their uniforms to shreds and inflicted festering wounds. For days and weeks on end they lived, ate, and slept on the narrow thwarts of their canoes.

Indian bullets were the least of their concerns. Heat, mosquitoes, exhaustion, and fever were the real enemies. One officer's report read, "Private Kingsbury [Marine Corps] fell in his trail and died from sheer exhaustion." Passed Midshipman Preble returned from a fifty-eight-day scout with his legs so badly infected from sawgrass cuts and mud that the Navy surgeon at Indian Key prepared to amputate them. Fortunately for the midshipman, who later became a rear admiral, the surgeon reconsidered, but it was two years before his legs healed. During another expedition, fifteen men died and another eighty became so sick they were unable to perform their duties.

One year after the destruction of the Indian Key settlement, McLaughlin's forces were almost doubled by the addition of three revenue cutters, a schooner, and thirty-five canoes. The new arrivals brought the strength of the Mosquito Fleet to about six hundred men.

By May 1842, it was thought that there were no more than one hundred warriors left hiding in the Everglades. The Army commander in Florida ordered an end to any further efforts to find them, and the Mosquito Fleet sailed home. As they weighed anchor at Indian Key for the last time, the crews' thoughts turned sorrowfully to the forty-five shipmates left behind who had died in the little "nothing of a hospital."

In all, McLaughlin spent a total of three years in the Keys and south Florida and personally led five expeditions into the Everglades. The secretary of the Navy wrote, "Lt. McLaughlin has manifested great bravery, energy, and zeal; and much credit is due to him, and to the force under his command, for the handsome manner in which they have acquitted themselves."

After the war, McLaughlin returned in broken health to his home in Washington, only to find himself facing charges preferred by a disgruntled marine second lieutenant. The lieutenant accused him of cruelty to the men by allowing excessive punishments and misuse of government property by allowing his wife to stay in the officers' sick quarters on Indian Key during a six-week visit. The secretary of the Navy dismissed the charges and ordered a court-martial for McLaughlin's accuser. The court found the marine officer guilty of insubordination and misconduct.

But McLaughlin's troubles were not over. A Congressional committee investigating expenditures by the Florida squadron made a number of allegations against McLaughlin, including unnecessary and extravagant purchases, collusion with a merchant on Indian Key, double issue of rations for sick men, misuse of government property, profitable speculation in currency exchanges, and improperly receiving pay as a captain instead of as a lieutenant in command.

Most of the charges stemmed from McLaughlin's proclivity for high living and careless accounting. His cabin on the *Flirt* was decorated with expensive furnishings, and he purchased fine liquors and wines for himself and his officers. He paid exorbitant prices for canoes and medical supplies but considered he had no alternative given his remote location and the urgent demands of his campaigns.

In the end, a Navy court of inquiry cleared McLaughlin of most of the charges but found that he had been extravagant in his purchases and negligent in his record keeping, might have profited from one currency transaction, and was not entitled to pay as a captain commanding. However, the court did not find there was sufficient cause to prefer any court-martial charges or recommend any disciplinary action. Two years later, doubly weighed down by poor health and his fight against the charges, Lt. John T. McLaughlin, intrepid leader of the Mosquito Fleet sailors and marines, died at age thirty-six.

With the conclusion of the Second Seminole War, the days of violence and bloodshed in the Straits of Florida and along the Florida Reef came to an end, not to be seen again until German U-boats began stalking their prey in the Straits during World War II. But the perils of the sea and the reef did not disappear with the end of the war. Men called wreckers continued to battle the elements and the coral heads for the rich cargoes of unfortunate merchant ships stranded on the reef. Their adventurous lives and daring exploits are told in another volume in this series on the history of the Florida Keys.

Glossary of Nautical Terms

bilged. A ship is bilged when a hole is torn in her underwater hull and she floods after going aground.

brig. A two-masted sailing vessel, both masts carrying square sails.

bulwark. A solid rail along the sides of the upper deck to stop waves from washing aboard and to prevent seamen from being washed overboard.

capstan. An upright cylinder-shaped mechanical device which can be rotated for hoisting anchors and other heavy lifting or hauling tasks. In the days of sail, the capstan, with a line wrapped around it, was rotated by men walking around it and pushing on poles inserted in slots at the top of the capstan.

careen. To heave a ship over on its side in order to scrape the underwater hull clean. Often done on a beach by attaching tackles (a system of ropes and pulleys) to the masts and heaving them down.

carried away. A mast or other structure on a ship is said to have carried away when it has broken and fallen or been displaced from its normal position.

carronades. Short, lightweight carriage guns that are effective at close range.

clewed up. A square sail is clewed up (raised to the yard) by hoisting on clew lines which are fastened to the lower corners of the sail. This is done in order to spill the wind or to prepare for furling (gathering sail up and lashing it to the yard).

close aboard. Two ships are close aboard when they are very near to each other.

crosstrees. Wood or metal poles attached part way up a mast to engage and spread the shrouds (lines that support masts laterally).

davits. A pair of upright cranes mounted on the side of a ship, fitted with hoisting and lowering gear to raise and lower boats.

felucca-rigged. A small, narrow-beamed sailing vessel with lateen sails (see lateen sail) (also propelled by oars) of Mediterranean origin.

foremast. The mast furthest forward on a ship when there is more than one mast.

freeboard. The distance from the waterline to the gunwale of a boat or the main deck of a ship.

freshened. Said of the wind when it increases in strength. A fresh wind is one whose speed is 19 to 24 miles per hour.

gunwale. The upper edge of the sides of a boat.

heel. The tilting to one side of a sailing vessel as a result of wind pressure on the sails.

helm. The tiller or wheel used to steer a ship.

helmsman. The seaman who mans the helm to steer a ship.

jettison. To throw equipment, supplies, etc., overboard to lighten a ship.

jib. A triangular sail set on the forestays (fore and aft lines supporting the most forward mast).

jury rig. A temporary, makeshift arrangement of masts and sails to bring a disabled vessel back to port.

kedge anchor. A lightweight anchor used to move a ship by planting the anchor some distance away in the desired direction of movement and hauling on a line attached to the anchor.

lateen sail. A triangular fore-and-aft sail, set on a long yard attached to a short mast near the top of the mast. The forward end of the yard is held close to the deck so that the other end is raised high above the top of the mast.

lateen-rigged. Having a lateen sail or sails.

leadsman. A seaman who takes soundings (measures the depth of the water) by heaving a lead line (a line with a lead weight on the end) and noting the depth by markers on the line.

leeward. In the direction toward which the wind is blowing.

luffed up. Turning a sailing vessel into the wind so that fore-and-aft sails are luffing (fluttering) in the wind and the vessel loses headway.

mainmast. The principal mast of a sailing vessel. In a three-masted vessel, the middle mast is the mainmast.

muffled oars. Oars wrapped with canvas or leather in the way of the rowlocks (semi-circular cutouts in gunwale to take oars) to suppress noise when approaching an enemy.

oakum. Hemp fibre from old ropes, treated with tar, used to caulk seams in ships.

passed midshipman. In the early 1800s, the next highest non-commissioned rank above midshipman.

quarterdeck. In sailing ships, the part of the upper deck abaft the mainmast from which the ship is commanded.

ratlines. Rope steps on shrouds (lines supporting masts) used to climb rigging.

riding bitts. Strong deck posts at the bow used to secure anchor and mooring lines.

schooner. A sailing vessel with fore-and-aft sails and two or more masts.

send down. To lower yards or masts to stowed positions, usually done in preparation for heavy weather.

sheering off. Moving away from.

ship. In the age of sail, a three-masted vessel with square sails on each mast.

sloop. A single-masted sailing vessel with fore-and-aft sails.

steerageway. The minimum speed through the water necessary for the rudder to be effective in steering the ship.

tack. To turn a ship by swinging the bow through the wind so as to bring wind from one side of the sails to the other. Sailing vessels must tack in order to make headway in the direction from which the wind is blowing.

taffrail. A rail around the stern of a ship.

tiller. A wood or metal bar attached to the top of the rudder and used to turn it.

topgallant mast. The mast above the topmast.

topmast. The next mast above the lowest mast.

topping lift. A line attached to the unsupported end of a boom or other spar to raise or lower it or hold it up when the sail is not raised.

triatic stay. A line running between the head of the foremast and the head of the mainmast to which hoisting tackles can be attached.

unmanifested. Not listed on the manifest (an itemized list of the ship's cargo).

veer. To allow the anchor line to run out.

wear. To change the direction in which the ship is headed by swinging the stern through the wind. Opposite of tack.

yards. Wood or metal poles (spars), tapered at one or both the ends, crossing the masts of a ship horizontally or diagonally, from which sails are set.

Bibliography

Introduction

"Letter from S. R. Mallory, collector of the port of Key West to the Superintendent of the Coast Survey, relative to the Florida keys and reefs, Washington, December 28, 1848." Senate Document 242, 30th Congress, First Session, 1848. Washington, D.C.: U.S. Government Printing Office.

Remarks by Senator Stephen R. Mallory of Florida. *Congressional Globe.* S. Senate, 35th Congress, Second Session, pt. 2, p. 1190, February 21, 1859. Washington, D.C.: U.S. Government Printing Office.

"Wrecks." *Key West Inquirer* (March 5, 1836): 2.

"Wrecks, Wrecking, Wreckers, and Wreckees." *Hunt's Merchant's Magazine and Commercial Review* (1842): 349–354.

Chapter 1

"A 17th Century Letter of Gabriel Diaz Vara Calderón, Bishop of Cuba, Describing the Indians and Indian Missions of Florida." Transcribed and translated by Lucy L. Wenhold. Introduction by John R. Swanton. Smithsonian Miscellaneous Collections, Vol. 95, No. 16, Publication 3398 (1936).

Barcia's Chronological History of the Continent of Florida, 1512–1722. Translated by Anthony Kerrigan. Reprinted. Westport, Connecticut: Greenwood Press, 1970.

Charlevoix's Louisiana. Selections from the *History* and the *Journal* by Pierre F. X. de Charlevoix. Edited by Charles E. O'Neill. Baton Rouge: Louisiana State University Press, 1977.

Connor, Jeanette Thurber. *Colonial Records of Spanish Florida,* Vol 1. DeLand, Florida: Florida State Historical Society, 1921.

Fontaneda, Do. d'Escalante. *Memoir of Do. d'Escalante Fontaneda Respecting Florida Written in Spain, about the Year 1575.* Translated by Buckingham Smith. Annotated by David O. True. Coral Gables: Glades House, 1944.

Goggin, John, and Frank H. Sommer. "Excavations on Upper Matecumbe Key, Florida." *Yale University Publications in Anthropology,* No. 41 (1949): 15–27.

Lyon, Eugene. "The Fate of the Florida Indians, as Recorded in Spanish and Cuban Archives, and as Particularly Related to the Florida Keys." An address to the Key West Maritime Historical Society, June 9, 1995.

Lyon, Eugene. "Utilization of Marine Resources by the Keys and Coastal Indians of the Pre-contact and Contact Periods." *Conference on Florida's Maritime Heritage.* Edited by Barbara A. Purdy. Gainesville: Florida State Museum, 1980.

Lyon, Eugene. *The Search for the Atocha.* New York: Harper and Row, 1979.

Missions to the Calusa. Edited and translated by John H. Hann.Gainesville: University of Florida Press, 1991.

"A Petition from Some Latin American Fishermen, 1838." Edited by James W. Covington. *Tequesta,* No. 14 (1954): 61–65.

Tacachale—Essays on the Indians of Florida and Southeastern Georgia During the Historic Period. Edited by Jerald Milanich and Samuel Proctor. Gainesville: University of Florida, 1978.

Testimony of Captain Don Martín de Melgar. AGI Contraduria 1115 and 1155. Seville, Spain: Archivo General de Indias.

Chapter 2

Account of rescue of crew of shipwrecked Spanish vessel off Key Largo by Bahamian wreckers. *Bahamas Gazette* (September 17 and October 8, 1785).

Adams, Eric. "Hurricane Uncovers 18th Century Wreck [HMS Fowey]." *Naval History,* Vol. 10, No. 5 (September/October 1996): 32–36.

Arnade, Charles W. "Florida Keys: English or Spanish in 1763?" *Tequesta,* No. 15 (1955): 41–53.

Connor. *Colonial Records of Spanish Florida,* Vol. 1.

Gauld, George. *Observations on the Florida Kays, Reef, and Gulf with Directions for Sailing Among the Kays.* London: 1796.

Geiger, Maynard. *The Franciscan Conquest of Florida 1573–1618.* Washington, D.C.: Catholic University of America, 1937.

Hammon, Briton. *A Narrative of the Uncommon Sufferings and Surprizing Deliverance of Briton Hammon.* Reprint of the 1760 edition. New York: Garland Publishing, Inc., 1978.

Log and Captain's Journal of HMS *Tyger,* January to May 1742. London: Public Record Office.

Lyon, Eugene. *The Enterprise of Florida.* Gainesville: The University Presses of Florida, 1975.

Minutes of Court-martials Relating to the Wreck of HMS *Tyger* at the Dry Tortugas, January 12, 1742. London: Public Record Office.

Nolte, Vincent. *The Memoirs of Vincent Nolte.* Translated from the German with introduction by Burton Rascoe. New York: G. Howard Watt, 1934.

Peterson, Mendel. "The Last Cruise of H.M.S. 'Loo.'" Smithsonian Miscellaneous Collections, Vol. 131, No. 2. Washington, D.C.: The Smithsonian Institution, 1955.

Report of the loss of the Spanish mail ships *Reyna Luisa* and *El Dichoso* on Key Largo in 1794. Translated by George L. De Coster and James Clupper. Seville, Spain: Archivo General India, Estado 5. Unpublished.

Swanson, Carl E. *Predators and Prizes: American Privateering and Imperial Warfare 1739–1748.* Columbia: University of South Carolina Press, 1991.

Chapter 3

Account of Captain Wimble's engagement with a Porto-Rico privateer. *South Carolina Gazette* (October 18, 1742).

Chapin, Howard M. *Privateering in King George's War 1739–1748.* Providence: E. A. Johnson Co., 1928.

Chapin, Howard M. *Rhode Island Privateers in King George's War 1739–1748.* Providence: Rhode Island Historical Society, 1926.

Cranwell, John Phillips, and William Bowers Crane. *Men of Marque.* New York: W. W. Norton & Company, 1940.

Cumming, William P. "The Turbulent Life of Captain James Wimble." *The North Carolina Historical Review,* XLVI (1969): 1–18.

Ellicott, Andrew. *The Journal of Andrew Ellicott, Late Commissioner on Behalf of the U.S. During Part of the Year 1796, the Years 1797, 1798, 1799, and Part of the Year 1800 for Determining the Boundary Between the U.S. and the Possessions of His Catholic Majesty in America.* Chicago: Quadrangle Books, 1962.

Garitee, Jerome R. *The Republic's Private Navy.* Middletown, Connecticut: Wesleyan University Press for Mystic Seaport, Inc., 1977.

Kendall, Charles Wye. *Private Men of War*. London: Philip Allan and Co., 1931.

Maclay, Edgar Stanton. *A History of American Privateers*. New York: D. Appleton and Company, 1899.

Marx, Robert F. *The Capture of the Treasure Fleet*. New York: David McKay Co., Inc., 1977.

Morgan, William James. "American Privateering in America's War for Independence, 1775–1783." *The American Neptune*, Vol. XXXVI, No. 2 (April 1976): 82–87.

Naval Documents of the American Revolution, Vol. 5, *American Theater: May 9, 1776–July 31, 1776*. William James Morgan, ed. Washington, D.C.: Naval Historical Center, Department of the Navy, 1970.

"Peter Norris and Others vs. Schooner *Polly and Nancy*." Records of Court of Admiralty, Charles Town, South Carolina, between February 11, 1778 and March 19, 1778. Collected and transcribed by Gail Swanson.

Swanson, Carl E. *Predators and Prizes: American Privateering and Imperial Warfare 1739–1748*. Columbia: University of South Carolina Press, 1991.

Testimony of Captains Flowers and Rouse and Spanish prisoners at a court of Vice Admiralty, held at Newport, Colony of Rhode Island, Sept. 30, 1742. *The Admiralty Papers*, Vol. 1 (1726–1743). Providence: Rhode Island State Archives.

Chapter 4

"Action with the Pirates and Death of Lieut. Com'dt Allen!" *American Beacon* (November 29, 1822).

Allen, Gardner W. *Our Navy and the West Indian Pirates*. Salem, Massachusetts: Essex Institute, 1929.

Bradlee, Francis B. C. *Piracy in the West Indies and Its Suppression*. Salem, Massachusetts: The Essex Institute, 1923.

Craton, Michael, and Gail Saunders. *Islanders in the Stream: A History of the Bahamian People*. Athens, Georgia: University of Georgia Press, 1992.

"Death of Lieut. Allen, Official Account, United States Schooner *Alligator*, Matanzas, Nov. 16th, 1822." Letter to Secretary of the Navy from J. M. Dale Commanding. *Niles Register* (February 1, 1823): 345.

"Destruction of Pirates." Copy of a letter from Commodore Porter to the

Secretary of the Navy enclosing a copy of Captain Watson's report. *Niles Register* (August 9, 1823): 359.

"Extract from the log book of the schooner *Mary McKoy,* Marcellin, from the coast of Florida." *The Columbian Museum & Savannah Gazette* (July 27, 1820).

Green, S. A. "Some Notes on Piracy" [Includes letter from the supercargo of the ship *Emma Sophia*]. *Massachusetts Historical Society Proceedings,* Vol. 44 (1910–1911): 453–459.

Green, Samuel A. *Piracy Off the Florida Coast and Elsewhere.* Cambridge, Massachusetts: Cambridge University Press, 1911.

Jameson, Colin. "Porter and the Pirates–The Navy's First Two Years in Key West, 1823–1825." *Martello,* No. 7 (1973): 5–34.

"The memorial of John W. Simonton, John Whitehead, and the heirs and legal representatives of Prudon [*sic*] C. Greene and J. W. Fleming, deceased." House of Representatives, 30th Congress, First Session, Report No. 189, February 9, 1848. Washington, D.C.: U.S. Government Printing Office, 1948.

"More Piracy! Extract from the Log-Book of the sch'r *Mary McKoy,* Capt. Morcelin, on the Coast of Florida, June 27, 1820." *The Georgian* (July 25, 1820): 2.

News account: Crewmen marooned on Sand Key by pirates, three perished. *Mobile Commercial Register* (April 25, 1822 and November 28, 1824).

"The Pirates of Cuba." Extract of a letter from an officer on the United States Schooner *Alligator. Niles Register* (December 7, 1822): 211.

"Porter's Squadron." A private letter from the commodore dated onboard *Sea Gull,* June 11. *Niles Register* (July 19, 1823): 309.

Record of the Court of Inquiry into the loss of the U.S. Schooner *Alligator* held onboard the U.S. Frigate *Guerriere,* December 13, 1822. Records of General Courts-Martial and Courts of Inquiry of the Navy Department, 1799–1867, Roll 15. Washington, D.C.: National Archives.

Wheeler, Richard. *In Pirate Waters.* New York: Thomas Y. Crowell Company, 1969.

Whipple, A. B. C. *Pirate: Rascals of the Spanish Main.* New York: Doubleday & Company, 1957.

Chapter 5

Bidwell, Robert L. "The First Mexican Navy." Unpublished doctoral thesis. Charlottesville: Corcoran Department of History, University of Virginia, 1960.

Long, David. *Nothing Too Daring: A Biography of Commodore David Porter 1780–1843*. Annapolis: U.S. Naval Institute Press, 1970.

Niles Register. Various dates in 1827 and 1828.

Pensacola Gazette. Various dates in 1827 and 1828.

Turnbull, Archibald Douglas. *Commodore David Porter 1780–1843*. New York: Century, 1929.

West, Richard S. Jr. *The Second Admiral—A Life of David Dixon Porter 1813–1891*. New York: Coward-McCann, Inc., 1937.

Chapter 6

Chapelle, Howard I. *The History of American Sailing Ships*. New York: W. W. Norton & Co., Inc., 1935.

Correspondence of the Secretary of the Treasury with Collectors of Customs, 1789–1833, Key West, Florida; Letters to the Collector, 1826–1833; Letters from the Collector, 1829–1832. Washington, D.C.: Record Group 56, National Archives.

King, Irving H., *The Coast Guard Under Sail*. Annapolis: Naval Institute Press, 1989.

Letter to His Excellency A. Jackson, President of the United States, from the Collector of Customs, Key West, August 8, 1829. *The Territorial Papers of the U.S., Vol. XXIV, The Territory of Florida, 1828–1834*. Washington, D.C.: U.S. Government Printing Office, 1956.

Letters to Officers from Secretary of the Treasury. Instructions to Officers in the U.S. Revenue Cutter Service, October 1834. Washington, D.C.: Record Group 26, National Archives.

Log Book of the U.S. Revenue Cutter *Marion,* October 1828 to May 1829. U.S.C.G. 111B, reel 97G. Gainesville: P. K. Younge Library, University of Florida.

Ludlum, David M. "The Great Hurricane of 1846." *Early American Hurricanes 1492–1870* (1963): 151–153.

News accounts of election returns. *The Register* (May 14, May 28, and June 4, 1829), Key West.

Proby, Kathryn Hall. *Audubon in Florida*. Miami: University of Miami

Press, 1974.

Record of Movements, Vessels of the United States Coast Guard 1790–December 31, 1933. Washington, D.C.: United States Coast Guard, 1989.

"Shipwreck—Reported Loss of the U.S. cutter *Vigilant* and twelve of her Crew." *Daily Picayune* (October 24, 1844), New Orleans.

Smith, Horatio D. *Early History of the United States Revenue Marine Service or (United States Revenue Cutter Service) 1789–1849.* Edited by Elliot Snow. Washington, D.C.: A Coast Guard Bicentennial Publication, 1989.

Chapter 7

Buker, George E. "The Mosquito Fleet's Guides and the Second Seminole War." *Florida Historical Quarterly,* Vol. 57, No. 3 (January 1979): 308–326.

Buker, George E. *Swamp Sailors.* Gainesville: The University Presses of Florida, 1975.

Buker, George E. "Lieutenant Levin M. Powell USN, Pioneer of Riverine Warfare." *Florida Historical Quarterly,* No. 3 (January 1969): 260–275.

King, Irving H. *The Coast Guard Under Sail.* Annapolis: Naval Institute Press, 1989.

Letter from Inhabitants of Key West to Alexander J. Dallas, June 15, 1836. *Territorial Papers of the U.S., Vol. XXV, The Territory of Florida, 1834–1839.* Washington, D.C.: U.S. Government Printing Office, 1960: 313.

Letter from Jacob Housman, Charles Howe, and William H. Fletcher to Commo. A. J. Dallas, Indian Key, June 16, 1836. Copy in history files of Monroe County Public Library, Key West.

Letter from John T. McLaughlin, Lieut. Cmdt. to the Honorable I. K. Paulding, Secretary of the Navy, U.S. Sch. *Flirt,* Key Biscayne, August 4, 1840. Copy in local history files of Monroe County Public Library, Key West.

Letter, Secretary of the Navy to Napoleon L. Coste, Navy Department, 10th August, 1838. *The Territorial Papers of the U.S., Vol. XXV, The Territory of Florida, 1834–1839.* Washington, D.C.: U.S. Government Printing Office, 1960: 527.

Letters from Officers of Revenue Cutters, various dates 1836 to 1841. Washington, D.C.: Record Group 26, National Archives.

Log Book of the U.S. Revenue Cutter *Campbell,* January 1837 to June

1839. Gainesville: U.S.C.G. 111B reel 15, P. K. Younge Library, University of Florida.

Log Book of the U.S. Schooner *Flirt*. Washington, D.C.: National Archives.

Log Book of the U.S. Schooner *Wave,* January 11, 1840–June 3, 1840. Washington, D.C.: National Archives.

News items on the Second Seminole War. *Key West Inquirer*. Various issues in 1836.

Peters, Virginia B. *The Florida Wars*. Hamden, Connecticut: Archon Books, 1979.

Petition to the Secretary of the Treasury by Inhabitants of Indian Key and Vicinity, June 1837. *Territorial Papers of the U.S., Vol. XXV, The Territory of Florida, 1834–1839*. Washington, D.C.: U.S. Government Printing Office, 1960: 405.

Record of Movements, Vessels of the United States Coast Guard 1790–December 31, 1933. Washington, D.C.: United States Coast Guard, 1989.

Report of the Committee of Claims on the memorial of Jacob Housman, deceased. House of Representatives, 30th Congress, First Session, Report No. 798, July 25, 1848. Washington, D.C.: U.S. Government Printing Office, 1848.

Revenue Cutter Services Personnel and Payroll. Muster Rolls, *Campbell* (1837–January 1838). Washington, D.C.: Record Group 26, National Archives.

Weidenbach, Nell L. "Lieutenant John T. McLaughlin: Guilty or Innocent." *Florida Historical Quarterly*, Vol. 46, No. 1 (July 1967): 46–52.

Weidenbach, Nell L. *Lt. John T. McLaughlin, USN: Mystery Man of the Second Seminole War*. Port Charlotte, Florida: privately published, 1995.

"William Adee Whitehead's Reminiscences of Key West." Edited by Thelma Peters. *Tequesta*, No. XXV (1965): 16–21.

Index

Illustrations are indicated in boldface type.

Here are some other Pineapple Press titles about Key West. To request our complete catalog or to place an order, write to Pineapple Press, P.O. Box 3889, Sarasota, Florida 34230, or call 1-800-PINEAPL (746-3275). Or visit our website at www.pineapplepress.com.

The Florida Keys Volume 1: A History of the Pioneers by John Viele. As recently as 80 years ago, fewer than 300 inhabitants tried to eke out a living without electricity, running water, radios, or telephones in the subtropical heat of the Florida Keys. The early inhabitants of the Keys will capture your admiration as you share in the dreams and realities of their daily lives. ISBN 1-56164-101-4 (hb)

The Florida Keys Volume 3: The Wreckers by John Viele. These true stories capture the drama of the Florida Keys wreckers, those daring seamen who sailed out in weather fair or foul to save lives and property from ships cast up on the Florida Reef. ISBN 1-56164-219-3 (hb)

Key West Gardens and Their Stories by Janis Frawley-Holler. Peek into the lush, tropical gardens of old Key West. Enjoy beautiful photos of the islanders' sanctuaries as well as fascinating stories and histories of the grounds where gardens now grow. ISBN 1-56164-204-5 (pb)

The Streets of Key West by J. Wills Burke. Simonton, Duval, Eaton, Whitehead, Southard, Truman—if you discover how these Key West streets, and all the others, came by their names, you will know much of the history of this little island. ISBN 1-56164-317-3 (hb)

Hemingway's Key West by Stuart McIver. Ernest Hemingway spent the decade of the thirties in Key West, the only place in the U.S. that he could really call home after he started writing. Also details his exploits in Cuba and Bimini. ISBN 1-56164-241-X (pb)